THE LEGACY OF EVE

DR. RODERICK LONEY

LITTLE ARK MEDIA
PRINCETON

The Legacy of Eve
Copyright © 2013 by Dr. Roderick Loney
Scripture Quotations are from
The Kings James Version (KJV)

ISBN: 0615845916
ISBN-13: 978-0615845913

Cover & Interior by Rock Spaceship Media

CONTENTS

INTRODUCTION

The Bible says that Eve was created for Adam to be his "helpmeet." For God had said, *"it is not good that the man should be alone, I will make him an helpmeet for him" (Gen. 2:18)*. Therefore, even from the beginning, God intended the woman to work in harmony with the man and under his authority. In a commentary upon this relationship, the writer of the Corinthian letter observed that *"the head of every man is Christ and the head of the woman is the man" (1 Cor. 11:3)*. This was the foundation upon which the creation plan was established. The man and the woman were made of one flesh. But significant changes occurred in this relationship when Eve yielded to the temptation to sin, and Adam followed her in the temptation. The Legacy of Eve was fashioned in terms of the fall.

Though Adam and Eve were of one flesh, each was responsible before God for his own action. God's warning concerning the tree of the knowledge of good and evil carried consequences for the individual who violated it. Before long, the woman did, and she became guilty before God. She had reasoned that "the fruit was good for food" even though God had forbidden them to eat of it. Adam followed Eve in the transgression having yielded to her blandishments. Both had fallen for different reasons.

The fall of Eve may have been stimulated by the observation that the animals which partook of the fruit did not die. For the scripture comments that she *"saw that the tree was good for food" (Gen. 3:6)*. In fact, the serpent may have called her attention to that matter. It would seem that whereas God was referring to spiritual things Eve's attention was directed to material things. She began to see the fruit of the tree as *"pleasant to the eyes"* and an asset to wisdom *(Gen. 3:6)*.

In the case of Adam, the process of temptation did not influence his judgment. He responded to Eve either because he saw no possibility of

1

life without her, or because he may have acted to mitigate her judgment. Whatever the case, responding to the woman had become more important than obeying God's word. It would seem that the very instant in which he took of the fruit, their perspectives changed. They saw each other as naked.

The process that led to the fall made it obvious that the woman had taken initiatives, which were not within her authority. The primary role in the relationship of Adam and Eve was assigned to the man. He was the firstborn. The right of primogeniture belonged to him. The supporting role was given to the woman. She was created to be his helpmeet. Like all other creatures, the man and the woman were empowered to bring forth life. But because they were unique creations, made in the image of God, and formed by His hands, the lives they brought forth were also unique like they were. Every child born of man is made in the image of God just like Adam and Eve.

Before the fall, the only limits to the freedom of Adam and Eve in Eden had reference to the forbidden tree. God had said to them, "*of the tree of the knowledge of good and evil thou shalt not eat of it*" (Gen.2:17). But now, both Adam and Eve had disobeyed God. Therefore, their roles were modified. Their paths became more difficult. To the woman God had also said, "*I will greatly multiply thy sorrow and thy conception...and thy desire shall be to thy husband and he shall rule over thee*" (Gen. 3:16).

Now, the fall had changed everything. The routines of life in Eden changed dramatically. God and man were no longer in fellowship and Adam and Eve had come under the power of death: their days were numbered. But God had taken steps to establish an alternative life plan. By it, the judgment of death could be reversed. So God went seeking after Adam "*in the cool of the day*" (Gen.3:8). He took on attributes of man, "walking" and "talking" in a manner that He could communicate with the man.

All things considered, God's intervention put man's life-plan on a different track. The fall of Adam and Eve raised up new life consequences for all men. But this study is focused upon the legacy left by Eve given the role that she had begun to play in the life of man and the relationship with God. Advances in communication have brought men everywhere closer together. Arm in arm with these advances is the rapid increase of knowledge and the expanding influence of sensuous relationships between men and women. The advent of communication that knows no boundaries has transformed the world into a Global Village.

Traditionally, most societies are male-dominant. But a tidal wave of social change and cultural adjustments have been sweeping over the world and transforming it into a female-dominant society. Everywhere women now seem to be motivated by compulsions for *"sameness or sharing the responsibilities of men"* There is a growing urgency for access to all of the same rights and privileges available to men. The *"Women's Liberation Movements"* and the struggle of women to fill traditional male roles have sent shock waves through the church as well. Here there continues to be a rising clamor for *"sameness"* of opportunity. It grows louder every day.

The Legacy passed on by Eve has tended to highlight her disobedience and revolt against the authority of God and man. Over time, there has developed a rising revolution that strives to overturn completely, God's order of things especially with reference to male and female relationships. Every effort is being made it seems to establish new guidelines for living for men and women. The emphasis is upon gender neutrality and sexual independence that often blurs moral and social constraints.

In many respects, a new feminism has arisen. It has become increasingly aggressive, bullying and even at times strident. Many of the daughters of Eve continue to set the tone for the relationships between men and women. One might even say in some respects, men seem to be becoming increasingly feminized and women masculinized. Terms like *"getting even*" or "*the liberated woman*" or "*gender neutrality*" have all become regular frames-of-reference in Western thought. In this regard, Women's Movements in the U.S.A. have continued to serve as beacons of "greater expectation" for women all the world over.

As recently as a few weeks ago a young woman planning marriage, requested that the vows be changed to exclude the word "*obey*" as it relates to the woman. She reasoned that she could not in good conscience agree to what that word implied. "*To obey should be mutual,*" she said. On the face of it, this request is quite reasonable. But its intent strikes at the very heart of the sexual distinctions established by God and the assignments that accompany them.

In the rush to demand change, the beauty and sanctity of male-female relationships are often misunderstood. Today's world is confronted with a new morality. But man's perceived needs must not continue to have precedence over the authority of Jehovah God. The church must find ways to distance itself from this "*new morality*" and its new theology. In this study significant elements of Eve's Legacy, will be reviewed in order to create a better climate of understanding of the roles of men and women for which God has prepared them both.

The issues under consideration in this study relate directly to questions of authority in all human relationships especially in the church. They will seek to consider the role of women as defined by God in the light of Eve's legacy. The author will review the elements of Eve's Legacy that have a sustained impact in the lives of the men and women of every generation. It is hoped that the findings will create a climate of understanding, which will contribute to better relationships between men and women in the workplace and in their mutual relationships with God.

CHAPTER 1

Contemplating an alternative to the word of God

The Bible says that, *"the man is not of the woman but the woman of the man. Neither was the man created for the woman but the woman for the man"* (*1 Cor.11:8, 9*). There is no viable alternative to the framework for living, which God has established. It is not by accident that God used two different processes for creating the man and the woman. Adam and Eve were designed to fulfill different functions. Each had a different role in fulfilling God's assignment. Adam was *"Ish"* and Eve was *"Ishshah."* However, when the serpent came along Eve began to consider alternatives to God's Will and Purpose.

Beyond the distinction of names there seemed to be an element in the nature of the woman that made her an easier target for the wiles of the serpent. The Bible emphasizes that the man, *"is the image and glory of God, but the woman is the glory of the man"* (*1 Cor. 11:7b*). Could it be that the primary heritage of Eve was enshrined in the fact that she was designed for the glory of the man?

The creation model set the tone for living for the man and for the woman. But God created the woman after he had established a well-defined relationship with man. Their roles were clearly defined by nature as well. Between them, there was little scope for interchange of basic responsibilities. Adam had expressed his satisfaction when God presented him with Eve. In her, Adam found the measure of fulfillment that he needed. He could now enter into conversation with one of his kind. Speech was developed and social skills.

There was no room in God's creation plan for alternative sexual roles. All such aberrations would be a result of man's fallen condition. Transgender was not a part of God's primary creation agenda.

5

Transvestites would have been incapable of obeying God's command to *"be fruitful and multiply and replenish the earth" (Gen.1: 28)*. For persons whose sexual identity was not well-defined God would provide other alternatives.

Eve had come to Eden. She entered the life of Adam and joined with him in a life of fellowship with God. But, the serpent who was present all along was able to draw her into conversations with himself. She may not have been aware of his subtle nature and her own vulnerability. But her presence made it possible for the man to fulfill his role completely. Also, the Bible says, that the woman is "the weaker vessel." Did her presence make them both more vulnerable to temptation?

It is likely that Adam and Eve continued in fellowship with God in Eden for quite some time before the fall. All indications are that their walk with God was satisfactory for awhile. However, it should be understood that they were not yet ready to be fruitful and multiply, since their standing was not yet fully defined. At this point in their relationship, man had not yet developed a sense of personal morality. Even physical nakedness did not create diversion of interests. The scriptures say that, *"they were both naked the man and his wife and they were not ashamed" (Gen.2:25)*.

The presence of the serpent changed everything. The woman had begun to lend an ear to his intrigue. In due course, his words began to be more significant than the Word of God. It does appear that this serpent possessed powers beyond those of a mere snake. Everything indicates that the fallen angel Lucifer was in control. In due course, he was able to influence the woman to put her trust in him.

None of the experiences of Adam and Eve up to this time had prepared them for their conversations with the serpent. God had not required of them to take the initiative on such matters. Their complete life-plan rested upon obeying God's Word. Each had the capacity to obey or disobey. But during her dialogue with the serpent, Eve's perceptions changed and she disobeyed God. She was not content to remain alone in disobedience. She shared of the fruit with the man to whom she was bonded and he too disobeyed. The deed was done. The serpent had gained the mastery, Adam and Eve had sinned.

As one reviews the fall of Eve it becomes obvious that her ultimate decision was based upon her perception of truth. She had set aside the judgment of God and replaced it with the judgment of man. The basis upon which she acted in each case was driven by her limited human capacity to make judgments that satisfied her own perceived needs. The established boundaries for living in fellowship with God were ignored. In all respects, the coming of the woman had brought joy to the heart of the man, but with it came sorrow and distress. Because of the woman created for the man, they would both be tested by God's boundaries. Adam and Eve were free but limited. Eventually, they were turned around and overcome by their passions.

Tested by God's Boundaries

The one-fleshing of Adam and Eve did not neutralize their responsibilities as individuals. Each was free to make personal decisions independent of each other. However, in due course the boundaries established by God seemed somewhat confining to Eve. What the serpent began to say about the forbidden tree made a lot of sense to her. The basic curiosity of the woman fuelled her communication with the serpent.

Before the fall, Adam and Eve were morally pure and well informed about life in the natural world. They were joined together as adults nurtured by God and not by man. There were no other human associations to threaten their relationship with each other. There was no one else to compete for their love and affection. Adam and Eve were the only ones of their kind. The process of one-fleshing is intended to do just that, create a bond, which joins one man and one woman in a unique relationship.

God had provided the man and the woman with all the tools needed for vibrant living in the natural world. But these did not in any way repress their capacity for healthy fellowship with Him. It is obvious that they were quite familiar with all of the living things within the garden. They experienced no difficulty in the maintenance of life before the fall. Conversations with the serpent were nothing unusual. It also seems that both the man and his wife were well-informed about the treasures that were hidden in the earth beneath their feet. Later on, the scripture speaks of the development of skills in music and metallurgy as well as farming and animal husbandry. All these things were tributes to the vast scope of information that Adam and Eve possessed.

As the man had fellowship with God, so too the range of that fellowship expanded when the woman came along. It would have been difficult for the man to maintain the same level of the Divine relationship after he had access to one of his kind. Both Adam and Eve were in communion with God but their lives were lived everyday in the natural setting of Eden.

The routines for living would have changed when Eve arrived. Her conversations with the serpent opened up avenues of thought that seemed to question the integrity of God. Continuing contact with the serpent was bound to have an impact on other relationships. There can be no doubt that the serpent conversations of Eve exerted some influence on her relationship with her husband. But the personal life bond, which developed, made it possible for Adam to say to God later on "*the woman whom thou gavest to be with me she gave me of the tree and I did eat*" (*Gen.3:13*).

The serpent was well aware of the strength of the bond that existed between Adam and Eve. He would be sensitive also to Adam's knowledge of his character. Therefore, Eve was an easier mark for his designs. It is not by accident that he began to direct all of the critical questions to her. In addition, his emphasis was upon what God had said, and what that might mean. The serpent knew that the strength of the relationship between God and man was maintained by God's Word. Thus, Satan began by asking, *"hath God said?"* Eventually, significant questions arose with respect to the tree of the knowledge of good and evil. God had said that it was forbidden. Satan set out to demonstrate that it should not be off limits to Adam and Eve.

From the outset, God knew that the forbidden tree possessed qualities that would be appealing to the natural appetites of men. But God's emphasis was upon obedience. God had said that disobedience would bring death. However, the serpent kept on saying that disobedience could not bring death. Eve herself had come to place where she *"saw that the tree was good for food" (Gen. 3:6)*. Thus, she was led to misinterpret God's meaning. The Divine reference was to spiritual death: but the serpent had deceived her. Neither Adam nor Eve would have been aware of this subtle distinction.

The serpent continued to indicate that the tree was a good source of natural food, and in all respects pleasant and attractive to the natural eye. His argument was persuasive. It is quite likely that the serpent directed Eve's attention to the fact that the tree was a source of food for many creatures, and none of them died from eating of the tree. So Eve herself began to think as the serpent did.

The word of the serpent had transformed Eve's attitude towards God's Word. Eventually, she yielded to the temptation, ate of the tree and fell into disobedience. With her natural eyes, Eve saw the promise of a new life in the tree even though God had said that it would bring death. Later on, she conceded that *"the serpent beguiled me and I did eat" (Gen.3:13)*. Eve had the mistaken idea that man lived by bread alone. This issue came up again when Satan tempted the Lord Jesus Christ. In His rebuke the Lord had said, *"Man shall not live by bread alone but by every word that proceedeth out of the mouth of God" (Matt.4:4)*.

But Adam and Eve followed different paths to disobedience. Eve had believed the serpent and rejected the Word of God. In Adam's case, he took the word of his wife and turned away from God. In either case, the deed was done. They had both, turned away from God, disobeyed His Word and eaten the fruit. Even though they followed different paths to disobedience, the results were the same. They were now marked for death. They lost their desire for fellowship with God. A fear of God began to erode all desires for fellowship. They began to experience feelings of guilt and shame.

There is good reason to believe that the serpent, which tempted Eve, was no mere snake (as previously indicated). He demonstrated knowledge of the vulnerability of the woman and her lack of moral awareness. He understood the power of God's Word and the frailty of man. The Bible leaves no doubt that it was Satan, (the fallen angel Lucifer) who had taken on the personality of a snake and tempted Eve. The writer of the book of Corinthians put it this way, *"the serpent beguiled Eve through his subtlety"* (*2 Cor.11:3*).

The process of temptation was no accident either. It certainly pointed out the distinct differences between the man and the woman and confirms the freedom of choice available to them. It is obvious that the tempter had carefully planned every move. There was no way in which the man and the woman could have withstood his efforts in their own strength. They sinned, when they turned away from the authority of God's Word. The fact that Eve was the first to sin seems consistent with the elements in the natural make-up of the woman. The subsequent fall of the man seemed as inevitable as night follows day. The woman was his helpmeet, bone of his bone flesh of his flesh.

The distinctions between Adam and Eve were not limited to physical differences. It would seem that all of their impulses and needs were also different. Thus, the serpent's approach to Eve may have had little effect on Adam. The differences in their responses in the face of temptation revealed characteristics that were unique to each of them. But the fall itself clearly demonstrated that each was vulnerable to the lust of the eyes and the appeal of the material world. God had created a unique garden in which to put the man and the woman. In it God had put, *"every tree that is pleasant to the sight"* (*Gen. 2:9*).

It was not good for the man to live alone, but the coming of the woman had brought sin. Even so, it is evident that without the woman the man's life would have been without a clear purpose. He would have been incapable of fulfilling the command of God to be fruitful and multiply. Adam and Eve were of one flesh. In every sense of the Word only death could separate them.

Living alone was not an alternative either for Adam or for Eve. Neither the man nor the woman would have been in a position to obey God's command. They were both as necessary to each other as life itself. Remember that when the woman was presented to the man he even gave his name to her. She was integrated into his flesh and bones. They were one-fleshed. Adam and Eve became one physically, spiritually and emotionally. For them one-fleshing involved a bonding with no alternatives. They were both committed to a common purpose, obeying the Word of God.

Though Adam and Eve were each responsible for their own decisions, they shared life in common. In such situations, decision-making requires unity of purpose. However, when Eve decided to disobey God, she was on her own. Adam was invited to tag along after the deed was done. Even at this early stage, Eve had violated the primary responsibility of a helpmeet. She had usurped authority of the man; she had initiated transgression against God (*1 Tim.2:13, 14*). The disobedience of Eve had violated the boundaries of Divine Grace. Now more explicit guidelines for living became necessary.

All things considered, the perfect natural man and the perfect natural woman in the perfect environment were ill-equipped for life in the material world outside of the framework of God's Grace. The *"wily"* serpent was well aware of the limitations of the man and the woman. He knew that outside of the boundaries of God's Word they would be vulnerable.

The fall changed everything, the fall of Adam in particular. The self-images of Adam and Eve were stripped bare. Their lives were no longer rooted in their spiritual natures. The flesh and its desires were now in control. Life as they knew it had lost its meaning. The pure love, which they shared before the fall was now changed, mutilated by sin. They saw each other primarily as naked. They became full of shame, full of fear, and likely, quite contentious.

Originally, the natural impulses of Adam and Eve had moved them to please God. But now the image of God in which they were created had become fragmented. Their relationship with God had also changed. They saw Him as someone to be feared. Subsequently they had to be driven from the Garden. Henceforth, access to God would be rooted in sacrifice. This was the heritage, which was passed on to their sons Cain and Abel and to all their progeny.

Because of the fall, new boundaries of behavior had to be established. It was necessary for God to make adjustments in the roles assigned to the man and the woman without changing their creation status. All adjustments were intended to facilitate them in their new relationships with God and with each other. The roles of the Firstborn and the helpmeet were restructured not muted. The Old Boundaries were *"redefined"* not removed. But, there was need for New Guidelines as well.

Therefore, God said to the woman, *"I will greatly multiply thy sorrow and thy conception; in sorrow thou shalt bring forth children; and thy desire shall be to thy husband, and he shall rule over thee"* (*Gen.3:16*). God said to the man *"Because thou hast hearkened unto the voice of thy wife, and hast eaten of the tree of which I commanded thee, saying Thou shalt not eat of it: cursed is the ground for thy sake; in sorrow shalt thou eat of it all the days of thy life*" (*Gen.3:17*). But, even though they had sinned, God had already put in place a system for reaching fallen man.

Free but Limited

The bible says that the woman was made for the man but she was free to make choices of her own. Eve had chosen, but her choices had broken the boundaries for living established by God. So, God put in place new limits to guide the man and the woman back to Himself. Both maintained freedom of choice but were limited by new guidelines. None of these changes altered the creation status of man. He was by nature a living soul made in the image of God.

Although the man was created before the woman, Eve was not an afterthought with God. She was an integral part of God's primary plan for man's tenure on the earth. But God had organized the process by a sequence of events not simply one act. It is apparent that man made in the image of God incorporated both male and the female elements. The process of Adam's creation was not complete until Eve came into the picture.

Each was assigned a different role with different responsibilities. But they followed different lines of authority in their relationships with God. The Bible says, *"for the man is not of the woman but the woman of the man. Neither was the man created for the woman but the woman for the man"* (*1 Cor. 11:8-9*). Thus in this sequence of Divine authority *"the head of the woman is the man"* (*1 Cor. 11:3*).

Adam exercised the right of primogeniture. But each was interdependent and yet independent as well. Each was accountable to God for his own action. Each was free to be and to choose within the framework of God's design. Outside of that frame-of-reference there was disobedience and death.

The fall and the entrance of sin strained the bonding in the flesh of the man and the woman. The scars of death were imprinted upon them and had a strong influence upon their relationship as they became parents. The differences between Cain and Abel the first and second sons of Adam and Eve reflected the conflict of values in the home. Whereas the first-born continued in a state of rebellion, Abel the younger was a model of Divine obedience.

When man disobeyed God, the spiritual connection was broken. He began to see with the eyes of the material world only. The first evidence of this was that, he saw himself as naked. But God moved quickly to reestablish man's spiritual connection. Adam and Eve had become sensitive to good and evil, to obedience and disobedience, to things carnal and things spiritual. Despite the reestablishment of fellowship with God, they remained vulnerable to the desires of the flesh.

It is not until some one hundred and twenty years later that Adam had a son made in his image, his name was Seth. The scripture observes that, *"then began men to call upon the name of the Lord"* (Gen. 4:26). Adam and Eve were bonded in the flesh and in the spirit.

1. *Bonded in the Flesh*

Despite the ups and downs in their relationship, the bonding in the flesh of Adam and Eve could not be rescinded or changed. All men and women are bonded in the flesh that way. The Word of God states clearly that even if a man is joined to an harlot in casual sexual contact he is one-fleshed with her, bonded in the flesh (1 Cor.6:16). Such a union can result in conception and new life. An equal number of male and female chromosomes unite to form one new life. Nothing can undo it. Such bonding is a symbol of the uniqueness of the marriage bond.

The social and moral implications of one – fleshing provide a safe haven for the nurture of children. To be one-fleshed or limited by the bonds of marriage is God's order. Anything outside of that is contrary to the will of God. On this matter the Bible says that, *"marriage is honorable in all, and the bed undefiled: but whoremongers and adulterers God will judge"* (*Heb.13:4*). The bonding of marriage provides a measure of assurance that growth into maturity will take place in a secure haven.

Soon after the fall, following in the footsteps of the rebellion of Cain, men began to violate the principle of one-fleshing (*Gen.4:19*). Polygamy, incest and same-sex attraction became widespread. Today these practices have become entrenched in human relationships. Too often marriage has become a charade at times, and, for the most part, a thin veil to conceal lust-driven relationships. Separation, divorce, and shacking up, have become the standards for measuring male-female relationships. It seems that all men strive to establish their own righteousness and set aside the righteousness of God. Reflections of the Legacy of Eve find expression in all levels of human relationships.

But the home has become an unhealthy nurturing ground for many children. In all such instances, the fabric of a viable society is eroded. As the Bible defines it, the marriage bond is terminated only by death (*Roms.7:2*). Its tenure is not determined by events, which occur along the way. As God sees it there is no place in marriage for adjustments by which the bond may be broken or amended. The Lord Jesus Himself made reference to it in a discussion with the Pharisees when He said,

> *"Have ye not read, that he which made them at the beginning made them male and female. And said, for this cause shall a man leave father and mother, and shall cleave to his wife; and they twain shall be one flesh?"* (*Matt.19:4, 5*).

But the question may be asked, *"How were they joined?"* seeing that Adam and Eve were able to act independently of each other. The Bible makes the answer clear at least in two specific areas. In the first place, they shared a common humanity, one-fleshed. In the second place they shared a common destiny, separated from all other primary loves, they were walking together.

It is obvious that when the Book of Genesis was written man had already parented. But Adam and Eve themselves had no earthly parents. However, the word was prophetic, setting forth the standards that should be followed hereafter, by those who were born of earthly parents.

Of one flesh they were then, before God, both Adam and Eve. Of one flesh they are now every *"Adam"* who is joined to an *"Eve."* But, the principle of bonding extends into all other areas and intensifies the foundations for sexual contact. In every case of bonding in the spirit and in the flesh the bonded couple is no longer *"twain"* (*Matt.19:5*). For practical purposes both would need to work at setting aside many of their initiatives as individuals in order to *"walk"* together as they share a common destiny.

Despite aberrations, many marriage vows in the western world today continue to include the terms, *"till death do us part."* In many other societies, different cues may be used to convey the same general meaning. In the natural world and even among some animals the practice of mating for life is not uncommon. But in the society of men made in the image of God marriage is more than mating, it is embarking on a life journey within Divine boundaries established by God.

2. *Bonded in the Spirit*

One fleshing for Adam and Eve had its roots in the mode of the creation of the woman. God had taken of the man's flesh and formed Eve. For all other persons sexual contact is the means by which one fleshing is actualized. But according to God's design, the process involves much more. For after God had created the woman; He brought her to the man and they were joined together in one fellowship. It is not until Adam and Eve were excluded from Eden that the man knew the woman in sexual contact (*Gen.4:1ff*).

The Edenic model of one fleshing represents God's design of marriage for all persons. The man and the woman who were bonded in one flesh were also linked by a spiritual bond. There was no one else in the world at that time with whom either Adam or Eve could bond in the same way. They spoke a common language, they shared feelings in common, in all respects, each was an extension of the other. Yet they retained the individual identity that gave them the power of independent choice. The physical bond provided the framework for a bonding of two souls.

In recent times, other sexual aberrations have compounded the confusions surrounding one fleshing and marriage. Same sex partnerships or loose sexual arrangements are no substitute for God's design. None of these arrangements can fulfill God's purposes in the spiritual bonding that must take place between a man and a woman who are one fleshed.

The Bible defines the boundaries that were put in place when the woman became bonded with the man. It incorporated both spiritual and physical elements. Such a bond could not exist between members of the same sex or with other living creatures (angels included). Any one fleshing that occurs outside of the spiritual framework is a violation of the person. The Bible describes it as fornication or adultery.

The Bible says categorically that,

> *"If a man also lie with mankind, as he lieth with a woman, both of them have committed an abomination: they shall surely be put to death; their blood shall be upon them"* (*Lev.20:13*).

The term *"flesh"* in Hebrew thought is a representation of the complete man. No man or woman can give completely of themselves to one of the same sex. Such relationships are a form of mockery. The essence of the marriage union is not found in either the rituals or the routines of fleshly encounters. It extends beyond these into the realm of the spiritual essence of the man and the woman.

The creation of the woman clearly illustrated that she was of one flesh with the man. She was not a replica of the man but a unit that gave fullness to his creation and completed it. For Adam and Eve one-fleshing was the means of giving birth to the woman. But for all others one fleshing is the means of giving birth to one flesh that integrates the man and the woman. Sexual activity was intended to consummate the process of one-fleshing not initiate it.

Outside of the boundaries established by God, sex becomes sin and a violation of the Divine code. It limits the scope and meaning of the common desire that should integrate and facilitate the journey of life together for that man and that woman. There is no other model that provides the opportunity for man and woman to replenish the earth.

At the heart of the physical process, which gives birth to new life, is the central principle that man is made in the image of God. Therefore, this new life is also made in the image of God and begins a journey that reflects elements in lives of both the father and the mother. But where there is no bonding except in the flesh, confusion often reigns with respect to the nurture of the child. The Bible implies that the new life comes forth in defilement (*Heb.13:4*). Outside of the spiritual bond one fleshing can hardly duplicate all that God intended when He created Eve out of the very flesh and bones of Adam (*Gen.2:21*).

Marriage is the only context in which the bonding effects of sexual contact will fulfill God's intent at creation. The principle established by the Father in Eden and cited by the Lord Jesus Christ is still in force. It is the only moral foundation upon which intimate male-female relationships could be built and common desires can thrive.

One-fleshing assumes that the interests and desires of each will become part of the common ground shared by both. It often merges elements of individual identity. But, it leaves intact the human spirit that continues to have the capacity for a personal relationship with God. The principles of one-fleshing are only in force in the material world. It is here that the man and the woman must seek to fulfill their Divine Mission. Beyond man's natural life there is neither marrying nor giving in marriage (*Matt.22:30*). The fullness of life on earth would have ended.

When Eve yielded to the serpent, she pre-empted the plan of God and violated the terms of her bond. But she remained one fleshed with Adam and drew him into rebellion with her. The fall of Eve and the violation of her relationship with God desecrated her bond with the man. Its impact created a dilemma for them that only God could resolve but none of these dissolved the primary bond with this man and woman together in a life-long relationship. Their freedom to act as individuals was only inhibited to the extent that it violated their bond of one-fleshing.

Turned Around

From the, very beginning the coming of Eve changed the routines of daily life for Adam. Eve provided the companionship and help that were unavailable to him earlier on. Now there was need for human speech and language. The woman also provided body contact. It is quite likely that Adam's relationship with God did not remain the same when Eve came along. When Eve turned to sin so did Adam. The blandishments of the woman had a greater influence on the man than the Word of God.

Eventually, the sin of Adam and Eve modified God's primary plan for the life of this man and this woman. Initially God had placed them in the Garden of Eden and put at their disposal all that the heart could desire. The Bible says that "*God planted a garden eastward in Eden...and out of the ground made the Lord God to grow every tree that is pleasant to the sight and good for food*" (*Gen.2:8, 9*). But now, they had sinned. The laws of living were changed. It was necessary that they be driven from the Garden and sustain themselves in a new life environment (Gen.3:24).

Now adjustments had to be made. The man and the woman were living in a new environment. The laws of living were modified in order to enable them to have continued fellowship with each other and with God. These adjustment did not come easily either for Adam or Eve. The dominance of the man became a sore point in their relationship. The daughters of Eve have chafed under that dominance until today. God had said that Adam would "rule" over her (*Gen. 3:16*).

Darkness was now on the face of the earth. Continued obedience to God's word became increasingly difficult for Adam and Eve. The fall had awakened the awareness of good and evil in Adam and Eve. The period of innocence was passed. The sanctity of the Word of God was breached when Eve began to listen to the contrary voice of a wily serpent. In due course, the serpent had done his work. The man and the woman were turned away from God, and all of living became suddenly turned around. Adam and Eve had come under the sentence of death. But God provided an intervention of Grace.

Sin had its effects on all of God's creation. Everywhere in the created world, codes of conduct were revised. New laws were put in place. Now the man, the woman, and the earth itself became cursed. Adam and Eve could no longer depend upon God for daily food. They were now required to fend for themselves outside of Eden.

The fall was bound to have its influence on their personal relationships as well. The new laws of God provided a different framework within which Adam and Eve would now relate to each other. Eve had become an ally of the serpent when she ate of the fruit and caused the man to follow her into sin. Each of them now saw the other differently and perceived of their own selves in a completely different light. Whereas the will of God was their primary base at the time of their creation, now, the will of the serpent became the prevailing force that governed their choices, their attitudes and their general manner of life.

For Eve, God had opened a door that promised misery in childbirth and uncontrollable desire for the man who would rule over her. Life as they knew it before was completely turned around. The responses of Cain their firstborn reflected an attitude of sustained rebellion against God. His parents were his only models. On the other hand, his younger brother Abel showed marked respect for God's Word. The influence of the fall and the chastening hand of God were making quite an impact on the general life and conduct of Adam and Eve.

The world itself had also changed: the lives of Adam and Eve were completely turned around. God was no longer their life center. The authority of Adam's rule on earth was now conceded to Satan. The Bible says that *"the whole creation groaneth and travaileth in pain together until now" (Rom.8:22)*. But the fall did not take God by surprise. The all-knowing Father had a new plan in place for man's redemption. The man continued to be God's centerpiece but now he was struggling with darkness. In due course, a second Adam would come in order to accomplish the full Will and Purposes of God.

Before the fall, the life-center of the man and the woman was spiritual. Now, it had become carnal. They were on the pathway to death. All of God's material creation was enshrined in darkness. But God had provided a ray of hope as He took steps to rehabilitate the man and the woman. The element of sacrifice was necessary to provide Divine initiatives for the man. The undergirding of the Word of God continued to provide the framework for fellowship. God's sanctified day now integrated God's eternal time with man's limited time.

The sin of Adam and Eve changed the framework of living in all respects. The impulses within the woman and stimuli within the man had changed everything. Other adjustments became necessary when the foundations of their relationship changed. God needed to provide an environment that would assist them in dealing with the inroads of self-will.

God's new directives seem to have blurred the operational image of the woman in relationship to her husband. There is overwhelming evidence of the despotic rule of men, which became traditional in some situations.

But there are also many examples of women in the Hebrew tradition who exercised significant authority in their households. Beside the *"Sarah's"* or *"Rebecca's."*

The Bible describes in some detail the life processes in the home of a woman called *"virtuous."* In Proverbs chapter 31 some of the elements of her daily life are summarized. She is described as responsible for meeting all the needs of her household. She is involved in trade and investments outside of the home. She is resourceful, diligent and industrious. Her children and her husband praise her and hold her in the highest esteem.

The life of *"the virtuous woman"* has not been the norm. Sinful men and woman continue to violate God's order. Bit by bit the lives of men and women began to seek individual fulfillment above a common life purpose. Increasingly each began to develop an identity that was in conflict with the principles of one-fleshing. Polygamy became the order of the day, and male dominance became increasingly overbearing.

All things considered, there can be no doubt that the status of today's woman is a direct reflection of the consequences of the fall. Outcomes of it continue to register shock waves through all male-female relationships especially as men drift further away from God's Truth. Today the advent of the *Woman's Liberation Movement* has put all questions of One-Fleshing in a completely different perspective contrary to the Laws of God.

But social change does not modify or limit God's Divine Expectations. Even with respect to difficult relationships where separation is sometimes advised, God's Word continues to say that, *"the woman which hath an husband is bound by the law to her husband so long as he lives but if the husband be dead she is loosed from the law"* (Roms.7:2). For all practical purposes, the death of one's spouse is the only condition that breaks the bonds of Divine "one-fleshing." Its intent is to limit human sexual relationships to one-man for one-woman and vice-versa. In God's order of things for every Adam there is one Eve. She is meant to be the only woman in the world for him. The Bible is specific when it says that *"a bishop then must be blameless, the husband of one wife"* (*1 Tim.3:2*) literally, "one and the same woman."

The intent of God in His relationships with men remains the same as it was from the beginning even though man has been turned around. The Bible says to all, *"Trust in the Lord with all thy heart and lean not on thine own understanding. In all thy ways acknowledge Him and He shall direct thy paths"* (*Prov.3:5*). Since all of the issues of today have their source in Eden, the case of Eve requires even closer scrutiny. The fall brought change. The relationships of men and women entered a different phase.

Contact between Adam and Eve was completely turned around when another voice entered the life, which the woman shared with her husband. It was the voice of the serpent. Neither Adam nor Eve was prepared to deal with it when they turned away from God. Conversations with the serpent may not have been unnatural for Adam and Eve; but his intrusion into their lives was disruptive even though all of the details were not spelled out.

What is included in the record of the Scriptures is only that part of "Serpent Dialogue" in which he began a commentary on God's instructions to Adam and Eve. The Bible is careful to note that the serpent was *"Subtle."* Therefore, he approached the subject very carefully (*Gen.3:1*). Because of his influence, all of the affiliations of Adam and Eve were realigned. He initiated a process, which changed for all time the relationship between God and man. Even the destinies of Adam and Eve and subsequently of all men were completely turned around because of the serpent and because of the woman.

1. *Because of the Serpent*

The Bible says that, *"the serpent was more subtle than any beast of the field which the Lord God had made"* (*Gen.3:1*). There is a hint in this observation about the role that the serpent would play in its relationship to man. It seemed to be the most natural thing in the world for the serpent to be used as an instrument in the design of the tempter. The environment of Eden emerged within the framework of time. Time was made up of darkness and light. Thus, the powers of darkness would have had access to the events taking place in the Garden of Eden. The scriptures say of Lucifer in another context *"thou hast been in Eden the garden of God"* (*Eze.28:13*). The man whom God had made became a prime target for the fallen angel Lucifer. He saw in Adam the opportunity to carry forward his rebellion against God.

Adam himself was familiar with the character of the serpent since it is he who had named the animals. This was not the case with Eve. But, neither of them had any knowledge of good and evil. Eve herself was quite comfortable to enter into dialogue with the serpent. It was not by accident that he first approached her. Before long, he was able to gain her confidence. His opening question was direct and to the point. It is obvious that this animal was also quite knowledgeable about the distinctions in character between Adam and his wife. Eve came to the point at which she "saw that the tree was good for food" (Gen. 3:6). It might well be that he had directed her attention to the fact that animals were eating of the tree and not dying.

There is no doubt that at this time Eve reasoned that the Word of God could no longer be trusted. She now saw the tree as *"pleasant to the eyes and a tree to be desired to make one wise"* (*Gen.3:6a*). The next step was inevitable. The woman had begun to doubt the honesty and sincerity of God's Word. In due course, her defenses were compromised, and, ultimately, she fell. Adam was alongside when Eve ate of the fruit and she *"gave also unto her husband with her and he did eat"* *(Gen.3:6b)*.

The activity of Eve in yielding to temptation demonstrated that she possessed a will of her own. Neither she nor Adam were robots: each enjoyed free will and ultimately sinned against God. But, by her action, Eve had violated the terms and conditions of her bond with Adam. She had set aside her role as help meet even at the risk of acting contrary to God's Word. The serpent was the instrument in bringing about the fall and also in turning around the role of the woman.

Because of the fall, it became necessary to change the ground rules for living. The relationship with God and with each other had now entered a different phase. The specific duties of the woman and the man were clearly defined. The woman had usurped the authority of God and man and the man himself had followed the woman into transgression. The serpent had succeeded in changing the lives of Adam and Eve and transforming forever the relationship between the man and the woman with whom he was bonded.

There is no record of the number of days or even years that the man and the woman may have lived in Eden before the fall. But it seems obvious that the period of temptation may have extended over some time. It may not necessarily have been confined to one day. Because of the serpent, life in Eden was disrupted and the affiliations of Adam and Eve were realigned, all because of the woman.

2. *Because of the Woman*

The Lord God made woman, *"and brought her unto the man"* *(Gen.2:22)*. Seeing her, Adam said, *"this is now bone of my bones and flesh of my flesh she shall be called woman (Ishshah)"* *(Gen.2:23)*. When the woman entered his life, Adam knew that everything would change. But, in the meantime, *"they were both naked the man and his wife and were not ashamed"* *(Gen.2:25)*. Henceforth, everything that Adam did would somehow be influenced by the woman. He continued to be able to act unilaterally, but for the man life was forever changed.

There is no record that gives details of the life of Adam and Eve in Eden before the fall. But during the temptation it became apparent that the woman was able to strike out on her own and follow her own initiatives. It is easy to assume that Adam should have been consulted with respect to decisions that would overturn the Word of God. But, it is evident that God allowed to each of them the measure of freewill that was congruent with personal responsibility. Neither could blame the other for acts of personal disobedience.

In some respects, one may say that Adam's walk with God was compromised when Eve began to listen to the serpent. The Bible says that he himself was not deceived (*1 Tim.2:14*). However, the evidence seems to indicate that he was present throughout the process and may have been influenced by what he witnessed. At any rate the bottom line was the same. Adam had fallen. In all respects, his life was turned around because of the woman.

In a comment in his letter to the Corinthians, the Apostle Paul made reference to the terms and conditions of the Fall of Eve saying that, "*the serpent beguiled Eve through his subtlety*" (*2 Cor.11:3*). Thus, step by step he had undermined her confidence in the Word and Promises of God. Even so, the results of the temptation would have been different if the woman had not given a hearing to a voice that spoke words, which were contrary to the Words of God.

It is sometimes said that the innocence of Adam and Eve contributed to the fall. But there are no conditions under which that thought should be entertained. We make moral choices because man's living environment is dominated by things that would stimulate lust and lead to sin. But in the case of Adam and Eve these things were not so. The environment of Eden was an ideal life-center, which was created by God.

The nature of man was not tainted by sin. God provided for man all that was necessary for living. Even the force and power of the wicked one was external. The Word of God alone was fully adequate to keep the man and the woman in a state of obedience.

There are some respects in which one might say that everything was changed because of Eve. However, it is important to remember that until Eve arrived on the scene the creation of man was incomplete. The life of Adam was also incomplete. Thus even though Eve was first in the temptation there was no way in which Adam's conduct could have been fully reviewed until the woman came along.

Two lives that had their beginnings free from the powers of death had become under death's control. Death became the destiny of Adam and Eve and dying their life process. Sin had now moved into the place of dominance. Their lives were under its control, the day-to-day experiences of Adam and Eve had changed. They had become bound by the Laws of *sin* and *death*. Later on, in His conversations with Cain, Jehovah God commented upon the way of sin when it is given control. He said, *"and if thou doest not well sin lieth at the door"* (Gen.4:7).

But Adam and Eve were made in the image of God, a little lower than the angels. Disobedience had severed their connection: they could take no initiatives towards God. But God could take initiative towards them. God's Sabbath was made for that purpose. It provided an avenue for the Eternal God to intervene in lives that were now limited by time. God had opened up a pathway of Grace. Yet for all this, the dominant rule of the man became the foundations of conflict that continue in force even today.

Before the fall, there were no rigid codes of conduct that regulated the relationship between Adam and Eve there was no "right" and "wrong." Rather it would appear that there was a comfortable application of the terms that defined their duties. Living for the man and the woman was a spontaneous expression of caring concern. It does seem that there were no formal guidelines, which determined behavior. But now that the woman had usurped the authority of the man, both of them were brought under the domination of sin, and new laws were put in place.

Basic elements in the nature of the man and the woman came to light during the temptation and fall. The serpent had begun to identify them. He pointed this out when he made reference to the fact that they were able to make decisions independent of God (*Gen3:5*). Disobedience would result in death Jehovah had said. But the serpent said it would not. What the serpent did not say was that such a choice would break their connection with God permanently. He painted the picture of disobedience in glowing terms, which all seemed to benefit the woman. She was deceived.

Eve was brought under *the "magical spell"* of a wily serpent. She lost a sense of the holiness of the God in whose image she was made. Therefore, Eve gave a listening ear to the serpent. In addition, it was Eve who tolerated his disrespect and lack of reverence for God. Therefore, Eve had concluded that God had not told her the whole truth concerning the benefits of the tree. Thus, she decided finally that the serpent was more credible than God.

The serpent had made suggestions to her, which highlighted several controversial elements, "*ye shall not surely die*," he had said. Also, he had said, "*ye shall be as gods*" (*Gen.3:3, 5*). These statements reflect the thinking of Lucifer, who himself, had aspired to be "*like the most high*" (*Isa.14:14*). Life for Adam and Eve was completely turned around because of the initiatives taken by the woman. Innate passions in the man and woman contrary to the will of God were stimulated by the serpent. In due course, these passions overcame them.

Overcome by Passions

God had created the man and the woman to be sensitive to life in the world around them. They were given dominion over all that God had created. In the perfect natural man and woman, these passions were quite alive. Their behavior reflected a measured response to the world around them. The Word of God had established boundaries that were not to be influenced by desires, which may have been contrary to the will of God. The serpent understood that. Therefore, the focus of his questioning was upon what God had denied them.

As the serpent began to question Eve, he asked, *"hath God said, ye shall not eat of every tree of the garden?" (Gen.3:1).* As the discussion continued, Eve attempted to share with the serpent God's reason. For his part, the serpent then began a process of demonstrating that the reason given by God had no foundation in fact. The woman was being duped but she had no way of knowing it. Obedience was the only basis upon which fellowship with God could be maintained. However, as she began to listen to the voice of the serpent her human impulses became stronger than her desire to obey God's Word.

In due course, the Bible says that *"when the woman saw that the tree was good for food, and that it was pleasant to the eyes, and a tree to be desired to make one wise, she took of the fruit thereof, and did eat" (Gen.3:6).* The woman's desire gave expression to what she had begun to feel. Soon her passions took control and her will to obey was compromised. She fell.

For Eve the fall was complete. Her passions had overridden her judgment and the Word of God was sidelined. For a brief period after the fall, Eve must have experienced the euphoria of eating of the fruit. Nothing else seemed to matter at that time. It may well have been for her a moment of passionate bliss. Spontaneously she turned to her husband and said in effect *"please share my joy."* But that joy was short-lived. As the eyes of them both were opened they were confronted with the impact of their sin.

There was no turning back then, as the passion of the moment faded, the reality of their condition overwhelmed them. Panic and confusion stimulated fear. They began to take steps to conceal themselves from each other and to hide themselves from God. There is a sense of desperation that replaced the confidence they had in their fellowship with God. All of the promises of the serpent were of no avail. They now knew that God's Word was absolutely true. The serpent had deceived them. A sense of guilt and shame overcame Adam and Eve the likes of which they had not experienced before.

Gradually, it became clear to Eve that she was led in the wrong direction. She had fallen, and now, all of her faculties were under the control of the serpent. Eve had become a sinner and Adam too. But Eve's confession signaled a change in her attitude to God. She was no longer hiding from Him in fear. She had begun to reach out to Him for help.

After their expulsion from Eden, the fall of Adam and Eve began to resonate in their own lives. Subsequently the lives of their sons were affected. Later on, a man named Lamech a descendant of Cain, boasted of having two wives and having murdered a man (*Gen.4:19-23*). The wages of sin had taken hold in the world. Still later on, in the days of Noah, the Bible takes note that men's passions went out of control. *"The sons of God saw the daughters of men that they were fair; and they took wives of all which they chose"* (*Gen.6:2*). Before long, sin became the modus operandi rampant everywhere.

One of the primary outcomes of sin was the distortion of the relationships between the man and the woman. A new dimension of living emerged. Women were moved to take initiatives that made them more attractive to men. The Bible refers to it as making themselves "fair," by enhancing their natural beauty in sensuous ways. At a much later date, the prophet Jeremiah compared the nation of Israel to a woman who took steps to make herself fair. She clothed herself with crimson, wore golden jewelry, and painted her face (*Jer.4:30*). The men for their part lusted after such women and sought them out.

Feminine appeal attractiveness became the primary guideline for relationships between men and women. Even the patriarch Abraham made reference to it on his journey from Ur. The attractiveness of his wife became a source of possible trouble for him. Therefore, he had said to her "*behold now I know that thou art a fair woman to look upon, therefore...when the Egyptians shall see thee, that they shall say, this is his wife; and they will kill me, but they will save thee alive*" (*Gen.12:11,12*).

Subsequent events in the lives of Abraham and Lot demonstrated how far man had drifted away from the Edenic model of marriage. Sarah's handmaid Hagar was assigned to bear children on her behalf since Sarah herself was barren. But when Hagar "*saw that she had conceived, her mistress was despised in her eyes*" (*Gen.16:4*). The events in Sodom and Gomorrah during this same period were even more far-reaching as men lusted after other men to the point of violence.

The sequence of events that were reviewed illustrates how the unbridled passions of Eve had come to express themselves in unbridled lust. Once Eve had given way to the serpent, she herself was no longer in control of her own passions. Later on, she expressed joy at the birth of Cain. But he became a disappointment and she expressed misgivings at the birth of Abel. The name Cain meant "acquisition." But the name Abel meant "transitoriness." The woman had come to Eden. She was created for the man, but before long she was overcome by her own passions and was the means of bringing sin into the world.

Summary

In due course, the woman arrived in Eden she was created out of the man and for the man. The coming of the woman created for the man had brought about limited alternatives to the Divine Will. They were both of one flesh. But during her sojourn in the Garden of Eden, the woman had moved from God's control to the control of the serpent. She had set aside the guidelines that were in place. Subsequently, new rules were introduced and the man and the woman were driven out of Eden. Henceforth, they would be the servants of sin, by nature irresponsive to God's Word. The coming of the woman had brought about a revolution in God's creation.

Initially, Adam thought that it was fantastic to have one of his kind, a real live person one-fleshed in God's design. But there was more. The woman was curious about everything. She had a mind of her own. Before long, she began to doubt even the things that God had said. Then Adam lost her. The woman had taken of the forbidden tree and was offering of it to him. This is how it all began since the woman was created for the man.

When Adam yielded to the voice of Eve, darkness had fallen over them; God's Light had vanished. She was a changed woman, he was a changed man. They were now both in each other's eyes. Their bodies became things of shame; they covered themselves. Fear took hold of them and they ran away to hide from God.

The coming of the woman brought change to all of God's creation. She could not be limited by God's Divine boundaries. She needed more freedom than God had allowed. She was turned around by the serpent. Driven by her passions, her loyalties to God and Adam had changed. Her own self-needs became primary. Adam was changed too, even their home was changed. Their world was changed forever and even God Himself became someone to be feared.

The presence of sin marked the beginnings of substantial change in the world that God had created. It transformed forever the relationships between men and women.

Sin established new boundaries for living. It made the man and the woman natural allies of Satan and put them in conflict with each other as well. Henceforth, pleasing God would require greater effort. It would not come naturally. Communication with God would now require that special processes be put in place. It would not be spontaneous. When Adam and Eve ate of the fruit in disobedience, even the natural functions of their bodies worked in a manner that was different from what was intended. The flesh was given the mastery over the spirit. The primary boundaries of life were violated. Male initiatives and female initiatives became blurred in the perceptions of fallen man. God's creation models had become distorted by sin. Death was now man's destiny.

But Adam and Eve were bonded in the flesh. Therefore, the fall had created new obstacles to harmony. Even the act of drawing her husband to her side very likely brought from him words of reproach and regret later on.

Unlike other living creatures, man made in the image of God needed to be specially- prepared for his helpmeet and she for him. The act of one-fleshing for Adam and Eve was a three-stage process. The first part was Divine. The woman imbedded in the flesh of the man. By a creative act was given the breath of life. The second part was socio-emotional when the man received the woman and gave her his name. The third part was natural, when their natural instincts aroused were and Adam knew Eve his wife. But at the fall, the instincts were aroused within the framework of sin. Thus, the psalmist would associate conception with sin, saying, *"I was brought forth in iniquity and in sin my mother conceived"* (*Ps. 51:5*)

Adam needed Eve. Without her God's plans for man could not materialize. But the coming of the woman brought change in all the spheres of life on earth. God's world would never be the same again because the woman came.

However, roles may be defined, both the man and the woman can only serve the purposes of God when they obey His Word. But the fall put all men in a state of permanent disobedience. To be one in the flesh with a harlot may be the response to a natural urge. But it holds back the benefits and privileges of One-Fleshing according to God's order (*1 Cor.6:16*). It violates the Divine Principle for the foundations of unity between the man and the woman. It short-circuits and aborts God's Sacred Plan for pro-creation. It puts in place a hollow mockery of God's intent. It is a sham that strives to parade itself as the genuine article. It is like *"fool's gold"* having the luster and the glitter but not the substance of a relationship that knits together the man and the woman before God in body, soul and spirit.

Through the disobedience of the woman, created for the man sin plunged the whole world into disobedience. If harmony with God is to be restored then the affiliations of all women and men need to be realigned with the authority of God even as it was with Eve in the Garden.

Adam and Eve were an integrated whole at the time of their creation. They were joined together in a unique way as male and female. The woman was present in the body of the man before she was brought to birth. The fall brought about significant changes in their personalities, their perspectives and their relationships with God. These have become the heritage of all men. All inherit Adam's creation status in the image of God but all are tarnished by the impact of sin. The woman came along and the foundations of the human society were established. But the relationship between God and men was changed forever.

Dr. Roderick Loney

Of One Flesh

So God had come where Adam "laid"
Keeping for the man the promise He made
Of making for Adam and Adam alone
A Help-meet complete of his Very Bone

Thus God made woman out of man
For that was part of His Divine plan
To bind them together make of Two One
Blend their Resources for birthing a Son

A Loose Arrangement was not in God's Plan
For that would just weaken and desecrate man
It might seem a Haven for Sexual bliss
But surely will leave all the Offspring Amiss

Rootless and trackless they'll not have a nest
A place to find comfort, a base to find Rest
For them each Nook or Cranny'll be home
A Berth, a Hang-out, a new stepping stone

Loose Sex has its hazards for women and men
A base of frustrations all "now," nothing "then"
Parading as love but only a farce
Concealing all truth by wearing a Mask

God's Plan is the greatest come weal or come woe
When all is considered it just will be so
No way will be found to offer a plan
More suited to meet every burden of man

Adultery beckons but that way marks Debt
And all Fornication is part of the set
One-Fleshed in the spirit is God's only Plan
For lasting relations 'tween "created for" and man

CHAPTER 2
Compromising the Truth

Both the woman and the man created in God's Image had fallen. No longer did they walk with God. The world around them had changed: Eve had violated the role to which God had assigned her. The serpent had deceived her with the promise of new authority and power. When she reached out to fulfill her fantasy, her connection with God was broken. The Divine limits were breached. So Eve reached out to Adam to share with him of the fruit that was forbidden. He also ate, Adam had fallen. The serpent had timed the process well. God's truth had been compromised by Satan's lie.

The changes in Adam and Eve were instant. It took them both by surprise. They had hoped for an upgrade in her status; but the promises of the serpent were only fantasies. The woman had reached out for something better; the man had reached out to sustain his bond with the woman. If there was any joy in the actions they had taken it was short-lived. The truth was soon apparent to Adam and Eve. They now saw each other as "Naked." The awareness filled them both with fear. Their world was falling apart. They had now entered the pathway of death.

The Voice of God which had brought comfort and peace to their souls now filled them with fear. The feelings of fear and guilt drove Adam to cry out to God saying, *"I heard your voice in the garden and I was afraid because I was naked and I hid myself"* (Gen.3:10). Keil and Delitzsch describe the changes in Adam and Eve saying, "The destruction of the normal connection between soul and body through sin" had taken place (pg. 96 Vol.1). Thus, the bodies of Adam and Eve could no longer be the pure abode of the Spirit of God who is the lifeline for Divine fellowship.

The man and the woman had traded in their freedom for a fantasy that turned out to be a nightmare. The countenance of God towards them had changed also. The Word of Divine grief and rebuke stirred in them a sense of guilt and failure. Over and over again Adam may have heard the voice of God saying, "*Who told thee that thou wast naked...? Hast thou eaten of the tree whereof I commanded thee that thou shouldest not eat?*" (*Gen.3:11*). What could Adam say, or Eve for that matter. They had no choice but to confess. Adam himself looked for an excuse saying to God, "*the woman whom thou gavest to be with me*" (Gen.3:12). But, Eve came right out and said to God "*the serpent beguiled me and I did eat*" (*Gen.3:13*).

All of Eden may have fallen silent after Adam and Eve confessed their sin. But, the Voice of God broke through the eerie stillness again as judgment was handed down, first to the serpent, then to Eve, and finally to Adam. Among other things they must now leave Eden and face the hostile world outside, condemned to labor until they "*return to the dust of the ground*" in death (*Gen.3: 19*). Eve's fantasy had hidden the judgment of God from her for a time. But, now both she and Adam must face the consequences of their disobedience.

Many challenges lay ahead for Adam and Eve outside of Eden. A way had to be found for them to provide for their own needs without God's direct intervention. It is certain that difficulties may also have arisen in the relationships between the man and his wife as well. Since they were both living in bodies that were tainted now by sin.

But God extended more Grace. The Bible makes reference to an eternal principle that guides the relationship of God with fallen man. It says that, "*where sin abounded, grace did much more abound*" (*Roms.5:20*). So God reached out to provide temporary cover for the sin of the man and the woman by the shedding of the blood of animals.

Although Adam and Eve had confessed their sin, the law of God was violated with respect to the forbidden tree. This act could not be undone and the consequences could not be reversed. So they needed a sin-bearer that would satisfy the requirements of God's law and lessen the severity of the penalty. All these conditions were addressed by the slaying of the animals.

When they sinned, Adam and Eve had died as God had said. But their death was two-fold, spiritual and carnal. Carnal death was not immediate. The full penalty was mitigated by what God had done. God had even promised Eve that she would be the mother of a coming sin-bearer. He would deal with the question of death completely by *"bruising the serpent's head"* (*Gen.3:15*). Their spiritual death was immediate.

Whatever regrets the man and the woman may have had could not influence the outcomes of their sin. The Tree of Life was now off limits and Eden could no longer be their home. But Adam and Eve were equipped for living in the material world as well. Remember, they were fully knowledgeable of earthly things.

Despite their knowledge, life outside of Eden was quite an adjustment for Adam and Eve. They were spiritual beings, made in the image of God and cast out into a natural world now dominated by Satan (the serpent's master).

As a starting point, Adam and Eve needed to learn lessons about parenting. The scriptures say that in due course *"Adam knew Eve his wife and she conceived and bare Cain"* (*Gen.4:1*). It seems that she was quite excited to receive *"a man from the Lord"* (*Gen.4: 1b*). Did she assume that her firstborn Cain might be the promised deliverer (*Gen.3:15*)? Sometime later, another son was born to Adam and Eve named Abel. Now the name Cain means "Acquisition." But Abel means "transitoriness," "nothingness," "vanity." Eve's excitement at the birth of Cain seems to have diminished greatly when Abel came along. In any case, things did not go well either for Abel or for Cain.

It is likely that the two sons of Adam modeled their lives on the examples of their parents. There was no other guide available to them. Yet, Cain and Abel moved in different directions. Their role models were inadequate. At any rate, Cain was a tiller of the soil and Abel took care of livestock. The lives of the two sons of Adam reflected elements of rebellion against God and of obedience. It is not surprising that Abel died as a martyr but Cain was a murderer.

Adam and Eve may have spent many days reflecting upon their lives in Eden. The world outside held none of the fantasy about which Eve had dreamed during the temptation. Life itself became a struggle for survival. Sin began to take its toll and many of their descendants followed in the ways of Cain. Evil began to gain the upper hand as violence and polygamy became widespread.

It is clear that the Garden of Eden was no longer accessible, but the worship of Jehovah was diminishing. The authority of Satan had become a significant threat to the authority of God on the earth. Before long, the negative attitudes of men towards God reached a high point and the days of Noah were upon the earth.

The Bible says of the people of those days, "*and daughters were born to them*" (*Gen.6:1*). It seems that for a time the number of women being born exceeded the number of men. This possibility could have contributed much to the problem. The prophet Isaiah also commented upon a similar situation in his day. He said, "*the daughters of Zion are haughty, and walk with stretched forth necks and wanton eyes, walking and mincing as they go, and making a tinkling with their feet*" (*Isa.3:17*). He also talked about their "*chains and the bracelets...ornaments of the legs and head bands...earrings, the rings, and nose jewels*" (*Isa.3:18-22*). Could this description be a reflection of the women of Noah's day as well?

Violence and rebellion also filled the land as every man began to do what was right in his own eyes (*Deut.12:8*). Thus, "*God saw that the wickedness of man was great in the earth*" (*Gen.6:5*). Echoes of the rebellion of Adam and Eve had become such a problem that God determined to destroy man whom He had created (*Gen.6:7*). But in the meantime, God raised up a man named Noah to bring to all men the message of deliverance.

Again, men were given the opportunity to choose between disobedience and obedience, good and evil, blessing or judgment. The outcome is well known. God destroyed the earth with a flood, and Noah and his family only were saved. The sons of Noah and their wives were challenged to make a new beginning. To them God gave a new mandate *"to multiply and replenish the earth"* (*Gen.9:1*).

As in the events in Eden so too, it was with the Flood. Whenever obedience is compromised and the authority of God is set aside, judgment becomes inevitable. But how could Eve have moved from Freedom to Fantasy? What are the elements at work, which drive men to reject the Freedom that God has promised and replace it with the fantasies that lurk in their hearts? The temptation that led to the fall of Eve had put processes in place, which led to her disobedience and that of her husband. They were constrained by the serpent. Now these processes were at work in the world everywhere. Because of the significance of the fall, the issues that moved Eve from genuine freedom with God to the Fantasy of sensuous liberty will be reviewed in some of its details, from critical steps to its consequences.

Critical Steps along the Way

Both Adam and Eve had enjoyed seasons of refreshing with God before the fall. All things considered, life in the Garden of Eden must have been perfect. Everything indicates that they lacked for nothing that was necessary for life. All that God had withheld from them was the premature knowledge of good and evil. Therefore, they were forbidden to eat of that tree. It is unlikely that God intended this arrangement to be permanent. There would be no need for the tree if it was not in the mind of God that they develop a sense of moral responsibility.

Adam and Eve were created the perfect natural man and the perfect natural woman. They were made with the capacity for knowing good and evil and the ability to explore these paths on their own. God's plan called for a delay in the process until they were capable of maintaining a position consistent with those who were made in His image.

Remember, *"good"* and *"evil"* were already in the world. The Bible makes it clear that both Light and Darkness were present from the beginning of the creation. But, the presence of good and evil within the reach of Adam and Eve did not really seem to be a problem until the serpent came along. He spoke of the tree as a potential resource center for Adam and Eve not a thing to be feared.

The innocence of the man and the woman made them somewhat like putty in the hands of the wily serpent. They were easy to be manipulated once they took their eyes off the Lord. Soon he was able to discredit God's judgment even saying categorically *"ye shall not surely die"* (*Gen.3:4*). As Eve listened, her thoughts began to stray. She began to doubt the Word of God. In some respects, Eve had begun to come under the serpent's control long before she actually took of the fruit.

As Eve began to drift, her conscience lost its sensitivity to spiritual things and the impulses of the flesh began to take control. Her defenses were broken down. Eventually, she came to believe that eating of the tree could in some way enhance the quality of her life. Remember that until this time there is no record of dialogue on this matter with anyone else besides God Himself. Neither Adam nor Eve had reason to raise questions concerning God's authority or His motives. For them, God was everything, Creator, Sustainer, "Parent" and Guide.

But, when the serpent intruded himself and Eve was receptive, the door was open for "dialogue" with the devil. The sins of Eve and of Adam also laid bare primary distinctions in the frames-of-reference of the man and the woman. Her fall came as a result of setting aside all authority besides her own on issues that seemed to be in her best interests. Her actions were impulsive. On the other hand, Adam's sin was a calculated act apparently designed to please his wife.

The personality of the serpent as well as his timing and general approach struck the right chords in the woman. Her response reflected attitudes that may be a critical part of the female character. Thus, Eve was able to review God's Word critically rather than accept it without reservation. Eventually, doubts began to arise because of questions raised by the serpent. Subsequently, she rejected God's Word completely.

The case of Adam was different. He too was influenced by Satan's overtures even though he was not deceived by them. But, listening to the voice of the serpent could have weakened his resolve to obey the voice of God. Therefore, he went along with the offer of his wife. The entire process had its beginning when Satan in the form of a serpent entered the picture. Therefore, primary issues to be considered in the review of the fall, is the influence of other voices that seek to introduce doubt in the Word of God and suggest an alternative course of action. Of specific concern would be the Content and Context of communication. Eventually they led to the conviction, commitment and condemnation.

1. *Contact with the Serpent.*

The serpent had the reputation of being *"more cunning"* than any of the beasts of the field (*Gen.3:1*). Could contact with him have been avoided? The answer is "maybe." But there was no apparent need for it. Conversations with animals were not unusual for Adam and Eve. Remember that he himself had named the animals at an earlier date. Also, both of them were perfectly blended into the natural environment. Remember too that Adam was given responsibility for tending the garden before Eve came along. Therefore, while it would be unnatural for men and animals to communicate freely today, it was not so when Adam and Eve lived in Eden.

The serpent's approach was casual but quite focused. In due course, he called for a review of God's demands on Adam and Eve. But his approach was one that demanded a reaction from Eve. He began by asking, *"Hath God said, ye shall not eat of every tree of the garden?"* (*Gen.3:1b*). There was no need for Eve to be defensive so far as she was aware. She did not even have a clue about the serpent's motives. He asked a question and she knew the answer. Therefore, it certainly was appropriate for her to answer as honestly as she could.

However, what Eve did not know is that on this occasion the serpent was simply a medium for a power that was far greater than he. Satan was at work behind the scenes orchestrating the entire operation. Thus, the serpent was able to project an understanding of the moral implications of God's instructions. All things considered, it should have seemed rather odd for the serpent to have an interest in what God may or may not have said. But, Eve was incapable of assigning ulterior motives to the serpent. She had no sense of any distinctions between good and evil.

After awhile, the serpent continued to shift attention from discrediting God to upholding the possible benefits of eating the fruit. As he became more eloquent it seems that Eve's defenses began giving way. Then the break came. There was a change in the tone of the dialogue after the serpent made promises concerning the virtues of the "Forbidden Fruit."

God had warned that death was sure for those who ate the fruit. But, the serpent now said that God's Word was not true. *"Ye shall not surely die,"* said the serpent (*Gen.3:4*). This was the pivotal question, "would she?" Remember that on this very issue Eve did seem a bit unsure of God's meaning. She had previously misquoted God saying, *"ye shall not eat of it, neither shall ye touch it, lest ye die"* (*Gen.3:3*). But God had said that death was certain (*Gen.2:17*). Her general attitude may have increased the leverage of the serpent in the discussion.

The full implications of disobedience were moved into the background as the serpent took steps to pressure Eve into taking action. Eventually, she would give way to the blandishments that seemed to be within her reach and take of the fruit.

The fact that Adam was not deceived implies that he continued to have confidence in God's Word. But God had made it so that each had to stand on his own. In this situation he could not have helped her nor she him. The status of helpmeet had reference to assigned duties. This was the first step in the temptation, gaining the confidence of the woman. The serpent had taken that step.

2. *The Context of Communication with the Serpent*

Because he was an instrument of Satan, the serpent was thoroughly knowledgeable on matters of good and evil. Eve was not. The serpent was also aware of the significance of God's Word. He was the mouthpiece for one who had experienced God's judgment, formerly, the *anointed cherub (Eze.28: 14)*. It is unlikely that Eve's prior knowledge of the ways of God would match that of Satan. But it was not God's purpose that Eve's obedience should depend upon her knowledge.

Thus, it was that on all points the serpent was well able to manipulate the woman with respect to any issue. The only basis on which Eve could have made a stand was by faith in God's Word. But, in the context of wavering faith the battle was lost even before it began.

In his approach the serpent began to put Eve's knowledge to the test. Without knowing it, she was walking into a trap that was carefully laid beforehand. On the face of it, all of the options seemed to be in favor of the serpent. But, Eve was unaware of the tremendous resource available to her in obeying God's Word. Thus, the serpent may have had all of the forces of evil arrayed against Eve, but she had the power of God on her side. It should be noted here that when Satan tempted the Lord Jesus Christ in a similar manner, Jesus' defense was always based upon, "*it is written*" a reference to the Word of God (*Matt.4:4,7,10*).

In the garden, Eve's faith began to waver. Therefore, the approach used by the serpent opened a door to Eve, which provided an alternative to the Word of God. In effect, he introduced her to "another way" that seemed right. The serpent offered Eve an alternative that seemed viable. He made it appear that she was under no compulsion to follow the path, which God had laid out. The threat of death was an empty one. There is also the possibility that the serpent may have called attention to the fruit of the tree itself. Were birds and animals eating of the fruit and none were dying? The scriptures say, *"when the woman saw that the tree was good for food" (Gen.3: 6)*. She must have had some evidence to determine that the tree was actually good for food.

Eve was deceived when she began to question the veracity of God's Word. The serpent had also hinted at the possibility of God feeling threatened by the potential benefits to Eve if she ate of the tree. As to Adam he seems to have been a silent witness. The scriptures indicate that he was present during the period of temptation, but apparently he was not convinced. The Bible says of him that he *"was not deceived"* (*1 Tim.2:14*).

From the outset, the serpent's approach served to put the woman at ease and encourage her to speak freely. However, the responses of Adam and Eve to the same information were remarkably different. Even though they lived under similar terms and had access to similar information, they responded in ways that were peculiar to each of them. Adam seemed to be somewhat reflective but Eve was more spontaneous and self-seeking. Both possessed the ability to make choices. The only basis upon which they made different choices seemed to be their perceptions of God.

But it must be emphasized that obedience was the key; that is still true. The Bible keeps on reminding the reader that, it is only *by hiding the Word in one's heart* that God provides the strength to avoid sin (*Ps.119:11*). Despite all of the ancillary support systems in Eden, there were no terms or conditions under which the natural man could have gained the victory over the *"wiles of the devil"* except as man obeyed

God's Word. Although Adam was not "deceived," he too fell victim to Satan eventually and brought down the world with him.

It is difficult to assign ages to Adam and Eve at the time of their fall. But, it is certain that God had created them of mature stature since there were no parents to nurture them. It seems certain also that their years did not begin to be counted until after the fall. Length of days only became an issue when Death entered the picture. The Bible also does not comment upon either the duration of the period of temptation or the length of their tenure in Eden. There is no way of knowing how much time Satan would have spent in communication with Eve before she fell. The Bible simply provides a summary of that communication and the context in which it took place.

Even though Adam was her mentor and guide, yet Eve completely overlooked the opportunity to benefit from his counsel. Also, if Eve was honoring her God-given role she would have sought the approval of her husband. However, she did not. Thus, the woman was prepared to usurp the authority of God and that of her husband. This was the context in which the serpent tempted Eve. She confessed later that she was deceived. She was completely overwhelmed in all respects as she tried to negotiate with the devil in her own strength.

3. _Conviction by the Serpent_

The serpent had succeeded in convincing the woman that his word was more believable. His approach had brought about the desired results. His timing had worked according to plan. Before long, Eve was convinced and took steps to get Adam to fall in line. This was after all the serpent's primary goal. Short of that, his final objective would not have been achieved.

For quite some time as the conversation continued, Eve was drawn more and more under the influence of the serpent. One would get the impression that she became sympathetic to his views early in their dialogue. At first it seems that Eve was attempting to correct the statements made by the serpent. But, this is exactly what he had hoped she would do. In doing so, she fell into his trap.

Perhaps the knowledge of what God had said remained clearer in the mind of Adam. He did not believe the serpent's lie. He had previously experienced obedience. Yet, he was willing to stand with Eve on this matter. Because of Eve Adam was willing to turn away from obeying God even though he may have witnessed her struggle.

She had begun to compare the word of the serpent with the Word of God giving to the creature equal standing with the Creator. It is obvious that both she and Adam were so significantly rattled and confused that neither raised a voice to refute any of the statements made by the serpent. Their own personal convictions seemed to evaporate. They became disarmed and somewhat defenseless.

So it was that in a "step by step" process, the serpent brought home the conviction to Eve that he was right and God was wrong. The serpent had presented himself as rational, likeable, and one committed to their interests. He wasted little time in moving swiftly to convince her that his ideas made more sense.

The entire burden of the serpent's argument rested on the thought that he was credible, caring, and vitally interested in the welfare of Adam and Eve. He relied very heavily on presenting himself as a person whom Eve could trust. As it was, he turned out to be untrustworthy. Thus, later on, Eve was able to say that, *"the serpent beguiled me and I did eat"* (*Gen.3:13*).

Most persons outside of the range of the serpent's influence would find it difficult to understand the tremendous pressure that the *Anointed Cherub* would have brought to bear upon Adam and Eve. On the face of it, one would expect their level of intelligence to be an adequate defense against the *"wiles of the Devil."* But none of these things are effective in withstanding the assaults of the evil one. Even so, at no time did Eve question the integrity of the serpent nor seek to disassociate herself from him. On the contrary, the serpent's heightened interest could have appealed to her pride.

After Eve was convinced, it is likely that the serpent may have lingered on nearby. He may even have pressured her to act with urgency upon her new convictions. It was necessary that she move quickly to bring Adam to her side.

It should be evident to the reader that the ability to make moral choices is not inherent in the nature of man. He needs God's Divine enabling. Therefore, it is only as a man draws upon God's support system that he will be able to integrate moral choices that are congruent with the Will of God. The sense of that which is **right** and that which is **wrong** even from the human perspective needs to be learned. But for Adam and Eve this was not so at the beginning.

Eve had come under conviction by the serpent. Therefore, she was willing to disobey God and follow the wrong path to the knowledge of good and evil. Her frame-of-reference became oriented to disobedience, sin, and death. Outside of the framework of obedience, all men are completely incapable of making right moral choices. Eventually, Satan had succeeded in convincing both Adam and Eve that obeying God was wrong and obeying his word was right.

4. *Commitment to a Course of Action*

As it was with Adam and Eve, so it is with all men. Living involves making choices. "Choice" influences destiny. The path that any life will follow is made up of the choices made. Some decisions have a greater impact upon living than others. Adam and Eve were confronted with a challenge, to obey God or to disobey. The results of their choice would lead to the path of life or death. Both Eve and then Adam chose the path of death. The choices of Adam and Eve led the entire world to the destiny of damnation and death.

Much has been said about the fall and even about the temptation itself. But it is important to examine more closely the point at which the decision was made and Eve was committed to act. Of all the things that the serpent had said to Eve, the most critical statement may have been that *"in the day ye eat thereof then your eyes shall be opened, and ye shall be as gods"* (Gen.3:5). If the serpent had added anything to this statement, it is not recorded in the scriptures. Rather, what is pointed out is that when the woman internalized this promise her perspectives about the tree were immediately changed.

Eve became committed to a course of action because she believed that it was in her best interests to eat of the tree. This thought must have impelled Eve to rethink her position and take another look at the forbidden tree and its fruit.

All of Eve's sensual desires were aroused when she reassessed the apparent value of the *"Forbidden Tree."* It became an item of greater significance to her. It seems that she was seeing the tree as for the first time, all over again. Now in her eyes it was a source of tremendous power. The Bible says of Eve that she began to see in the fruit, something that was *"good for food," "pleasant to the eyes,"* and desirable *"to make one wise"* (Gen.3:6). Eve was now convinced that perhaps her eyes had already begun to open.

Eve became fascinated by the benefits that the fruit seemed to offer. Therefore, she took the next step. She determined to have that fruit. The deception of the serpent was complete. Eve reached out to take the fruit and secure for herself the benefits that the serpent had promised.

When the word of the serpent became pre-eminent, Eve had fallen even before she ate of the fruit. Man's sensual desires are often the guiding principle in making moral choices. The lingering echoes of her fantasy were still in her mind when Eve invited Adam to join her in her sin. He did. There is no evidence to indicate that Adam had even hesitated. She demonstrated the ability to turn the heart of the man away from God. When the woman became committed to a course of action, it would seem that there was no turning back.

But, there are persons who seem to think that Adam and Eve were at an unfair disadvantage in dealing with the serpent. This was hardly the case. In order to follow the path that God had planned for them the innocence of Adam and Eve was a vital starting point. God was beginning His relationship with them "tabula rasa." There was nothing within them that could have hindered their growth in grace, no sin and no personal "axe to grind." Because Adam and Eve were under God's jurisdiction, their battle should not have been personal. It was the Lord's (*2 Chron.20:15, 1 Sam.17:47*).

As soon as the serpent had expressed a position that was contrary to God's Eve should have been sensitive enough to withdraw from the communication. Instead, she seems to have made it a personal matter. For example, Eve had said to the serpent that to eat the Forbidden Fruit would possibly result in death. The serpent replied "*ye shall not surely die*" (*Gen.3:3, 4*). That conversation reflected the final step in their critical communication. Yet, Eve did not turn away. Rather, she seriously considered its implications.

5. *Condemnation by the Word of God*

It is quite unlikely that Eve became immediately aware of the change that had taken place within her when she sinned. But, it seems apparent that her fall brought about an immediate change of character. She was able to move spontaneously in the direction consistent with her sin. She turned towards Adam and tempted him to follow her into sin. The works of sin had begun to manifest itself in Eve's behavior. She persuaded her husband to turn away from God.

51

It is likely, that up until the time of the Fall Adam and Eve had everything in common. They shared with each other. Therefore, it would not have been unusual for Eve to share with her husband a portion of her fruit. But since Adam was present during the temptation (*Gen.3:6*), he surely knew what the fruit represented. Any attempt to blame Eve for Adam's disobedience would be inappropriate. Each was responsible for his own sin. Both had violated the command of God.

The fall of Eve may have prepared the way, but it is the sin of Adam that opened the door for sin to enter the world. The judgment of death was not passed upon all men because Eve had sinned. God made a distinction between the sin of the woman and the sin of the man. The Bible says that, *"by one man sin entered into the world, and death by sin; and so death passed upon all men, for that all have sinned"* (*Roms.5:12*). The responsibility for sin is attributed to the man because he is *"the head of the woman,"* and head of the race (*1 Cor.11:3*). The world was his inheritance; he shared it with Eve.

When a person sins the lines of communication with God are ruptured. Some may comment that, since *"in Adam all die,"* perhaps judgment was withheld from Eve until Adam had sinned (*1 Cor.15:22*). Perhaps not, Adam and Eve were each held to a personal standard. God had given to each of them a separate mandate of obedience. Eve would not have been guilty of the sin of Adam, nor vise-versa. The sin of Eve did not result from a nature that was inherited from Adam. Her sin came about because of her own personal disobedience. It marked a departure from her condition of innocence. The separate judgments passed upon Adam and Eve reflected separate duties.

When Adam fell, it is likely that he had eaten of the very fruit from which Eve her-self had eaten. But, now everything had changed. His fall opened the door to complete catastrophe. The judgment of God began to manifest itself externally and internally. The scriptures say that, *"the eyes of them both were opened"* (*Gen.3:7*). They both became conscious of their changed perspectives. They saw each other as "naked" and "exposed," naked in the eyes of each other and exposed to the wrath of God. Immediately, they took steps to clothe their nakedness and hide themselves from the presence of God (*Gen.3:7, 8*).

But Adam and Eve knew well that there is no place to hide from God. When God asked the question, "*where art thou*" (*Gen.3:9*), the meaning really was, "where are you hiding?" The inference from that question is obvious; there is no hiding place from God.

All of mankind was condemned to die when Adam sinned. Physical death was progressive, but spiritual death was instant "*in the day that ye eat thereof*" – (*Gen.2:17*). The scriptures indicate that Adam's life in the flesh continued long after the fall. He himself lived for 930 years (Gen.5:5). The Bible affirms however, that in our days God has granted to each man a more limited life span.

> "*The days of our years are threescore years and ten; and if by reason of strength they be fourscore years, yet is their strength labour and sorrow; for it is soon cut off, and we fly away*" (*Ps.90:10*).

The *price for sin* had to be paid. Both Adam and Eve subsequently came to recognize that God's Word was true His Promises sure. Satan was proven to be a liar. He had deceived Eve when he said, "*ye shall not surely die*" (*Gen.3:4*).

Besides the penalty of death, there were surely other specific outcomes of sin in the lives of Adam and Eve. Therefore, God provided a way for them to have access to Him by means of sacrifice. The coats of skin, which God had provided to cover their nakedness was a symbol of the provision that He had made (*Gen.3:21*). God was aware that the thoughts and intent of the hearts of Adam and Eve would now be evil continually. Therefore, God made changes in the laws that governed their relationship and security was established at the entrances to Eden. The Bible says that,

> *"He drove out the man; and he placed at the east of the garden of Eden Cherubim and a flaming sword which turned every way to keep the way of the tree of life"* (Gen.3:24).

Adam and Eve left Eden as sinners under the influence of the powers of darkness. But, God's command *"to be fruitful and multiply and replenish the earth"* (Gen.1:28) did not change because of the fall. The Bible says that *"Adam knew Eve his wife; and she conceived, and bare Cain"* (Gen.4:1). It is not surprising that the wages of sin fell heavily upon Cain and he took a position of extreme rebellion against God even murdering his brother Abel (Gen.4:8).

It is likely that Adam and Eve experienced many hardships in the performance of their day-to-day duties outside of the garden. They were now the servants of sin, locked out of Eden and operating under new guidelines for living. Certainly, there was need to be constantly turning to God for aid. They would have surely needed to find relief from the hardships of living.

Because they had not obeyed the Word of God, both Adam and Eve were condemned by that very Word. But, the terms and conditions of their creation remained in place though now it needed to be tempered by God's Mercy. He provided the grace that was necessary to mitigate the impact of their sin. God also assured them of the eventual victory of man over the serpent in the atoning work of Jesus Christ. He had said that He would, *"put enmity between"* the serpent and the woman, and between the serpent's seed and her seed (Gen.3:15).

6. *Compulsion and Complicity*

When compulsions within us overpower the will to do the struggle is over. In the mind of Eve, the urge to have the fruit became a compulsion. Yet, she had not completed the sin act until she obeyed her compulsion and ate the fruit. But the Bible says of the sinner that even *"looking to lust"* is sin. In such cases, the intent is fulfilled because the heart of fallen man is at enmity with God. With Eve that was not so. She was in a state of innocence. She could not be drawn away by her own lust and enticed. She did not have a sin nature nor the knowledge of good and evil. Her thoughts and compulsions were the result of the doubt cast upon the Word of God.

The compulsions of Adam were different from the compulsions of Eve. Each came to the point of sin from a different perspective. Eve sinned after much thought and deliberation. But the sin of Adam seemed to have been more spontaneous. Eve reevaluated the dictates of God; Adam did not appear to do so. Eventually, Eve was fully convicted by the serpent's argument but Adam was not. Yet, in the final analysis, both Adam and Eve sinned but for different reasons. There were elements within each of them that responded differently to similar conditions.

Both Adam and Eve were driven by their compulsions. There was no evidence of other external forces that may have influenced their decisions. The Bible describes the outcomes of the temptation in the following terms, *"Adam was not deceived, but the woman being deceived was in the transgression"* (*1 Tim.2:14*). All of the information suggests that Adam was privy to all of the statements directed to Eve. But, he processed the same information differently. As a result, he arrived at a different conclusion. He responded in a similar manner to Eve for a different reason.

From the very outset, there were differences between Adam and Eve. Adam had heard the command of God saying expressly, *"in the day that thou eatest thereof, thou shalt surely die"* (*Gen.2:17*). What Eve heard was, *"ye shall not eat of it, neither shall ye touch it, lest ye die"* (*Gen.3:3*). Afterwards, in the course of the temptation, nothing was heard of Adam's presence but Eve was communicative with the serpent. She seems to have been more accommodating to the serpent and willing to listen.

Ultimately, Eve was persuaded to act, but Adam was not. He was present but unconvinced. Is it possible that the reputed subtlety and beauty of the beast may also have charmed Eve? All things considered, though Adam and Eve were bonded in one flesh they certainly were not one person. Their personal identity remained intact. But, would Eve have been willing to follow Adam into sin as he followed her?

Adam and Eve entered the world in different ways and under different conditions. He was created out of the dust of the ground and she was created out of his body. The woman was made for the man not the man for the woman (*1 Cor.11:9*). Adam had spent some time alone in God's presence before Eve was created. Also, Adam was assigned tasks and completed one of these tasks before Eve arrived on the scene. But her strength lay in following his lead.

At the time of reckoning, when God confronted both Adam and Eve, she admitted, but he refused to take responsibility. Yet, the Bible says of the woman that, she is the weaker vessel (*1 Pet.3:7*). No comparable evaluation is made of the man. But her weakness is often cited as one of the reasons for the fall.

However their differences may be defined, there can be no doubt that the distinctions between men and women lie at the very foundations of their creation. They are imbedded in the nature of the man and the nature of the woman. In the temptation, it seems that the man and the woman were driven by dissimilar preferences. Somehow, it appears that in the case of the man, the natural appeal of the woman was enough to turn him away from God. But, the turning point for the woman seemed to be rooted in the benefits that would be derived from the fruit.

In spite of Adam's willingness to fall in with Eve in the temptation, he was not reluctant to lay blame upon her in the presence of God. At no time did Adam demonstrate a sense of protective care for his helpmeet.

It is difficult to identify the source, which gave birth to the distinctions in the thought processes of Adam and Eve. From all that is known maleness and femaleness were the only things at the root of their differences.

The framework for living for Adam and Eve was established in Eden. But it is not until after the fall and their expulsion from Eden that fleshly concerns came into play. Their bonding in the flesh was unique since Eve herself was carried in the flesh of Adam before she was created. For all other persons one fleshing would be consummated at the point of sexual contact (*1 Cor.6:16*). Eve had come along as "part two" in God's creation of man.

There is no indication of the quality of daily life for them as it was lived in Eden. Relationships on a daily basis were not recorded. However, it seems obvious that Adam and Eve looked at each other with the eyes of flesh for the first time after the fall. It is then that they became ashamed of each other and covered themselves (Gen.3:7).

Could Eve have found it easier to accept the promises of the serpent because of the opportunity it offered to free her up from authoritative controls? He had said to her that, "*your eyes shall be opened and you shall be as gods, knowing good and evil*" (*Gen.3:5*). As Eve began listening to the serpent, she would have found it easier to turn away from obedience. The freedoms promised by the serpent appealed to everything within her physical nature. Her sensual compulsions came into play.

Eve's fall and the Judgment passed upon her, struck at the very foundations of her fleshly nature. She had rebelled against the authority of man and the authority of God. Now her revised status was designed to put her more completely under the domination of the man. God had said to her, "*thy desire shall be to thy husband and he shall rule over thee*" (*Gen.3:16*). Her place as Adam's helpmeet was reinforced.

Once she moved away from dependence upon the Word, Eve became vulnerable. She admitted very freely that, *"The serpent beguiled me and I did eat"* (*Gen.3:13*). She had no prior knowledge of the true identity of the serpent but his offer was attractive. She found his promises to be very appealing to elements within her. Paul makes reference to this event, when he said to the brethren at Corinth, *"I fear, lest by any means, as the serpent beguiled Eve through his subtilty, so your minds should be corrupted from the simplicity that is in Christ"* (*2 Cor.11:3*). Eve had come under the pull of her own natural compulsions once she turned her eyes away from God. These became more effective in shaping her behavior than anything, which God had said.

The distinct differences in the natural make-up of the man and the woman were the foundations of equality. The elements at work within Eve as well as those at work within Adam were consistent with the purposes for which each was created. The man seemed stoical in resisting the arguments of the serpent, but cowardly in the reason which he advanced for his sin. The woman seemed to be more easily swayed, carried away, hoodwinked, or simply fooled by a persuasive, *fast-talking serpent*. But, she was more forthright and honest in the reason given for her fall.

The Bible does not comment upon the underlying causes for the fall of Adam and Eve. All of the best guesses are simply speculative. But with respect to the woman, could it be that these distinctions are adequately defined when the Bible describes the wife as the *weaker vessel* (*1 Pet.3:7*)? However, one may apply meaning, it is clear that under the pressure of temptation God's Divine order was compromised by both Adam and Eve each for a different reason. Because of the sin of Eve, man was deceived. He substituted his Freedom of Fellowship with God for the Fantasy of Sensual Freedom.

Consequences of Usurping Authority

The fall of Adam and Eve brought sin and death into God's creation. There were primary and secondary consequences to the woman usurping the authority of the man. The full scope of that judgment is still in progress. God's entire creation is still literally groaning and travailing *"in pain together until now"* (*Roms.8:22*). But, God has provided another way, a plan for man's salvation. Because the first Adam had failed, God brought the Second Adam to the rescue. The Bible says that the First Adam *"is of the earth, earthy."* But the Second Adam is the Lord God from heaven, even Jesus Christ (*1 Cor.15:47*). His plan of salvation provided the foundation for the judgment of the serpent (*Rev.20:10*).

Among the primary outcomes of the fall was the expulsion from Eden. Adam and Eve no longer had access to the Tree of Life after the fall. They were excluded from the garden entirely. A special network of angelic beings was placed as guardians of the tree (Gen.3:24). The life of God that was accessible to them was no longer within their normal range. Special conditions had to be put in place to allow for limited access into the Divine presence.

Adam and Eve understood that each had a responsibility to obey God's Word. Their bonding in one flesh was under God's authority. But, it did not take precedence over their personal responsibility. Yet, it was not in the plan or purpose of God to deprive them of the opportunity to enjoy all of the blessings of Eden. God's plan had such things factored in at a time of greater maturity. Remember that the Tree of Life was in the garden as well and they were not denied access to it. It was intended to be accessible to them. The Bible reminds all men that *"to him that overcometh will I give to eat of the tree of life which is in the midst of the paradise of God"* (*Rev.2:7*).

But, the attention of the man and woman was directed to the forbidden tree and away from the tree of life. That which was forbidden became the very thing that preoccupied much of their thoughts and interests.

It needs to be repeated that temptation follows a path that is similar to the one taken by Adam and Eve. The Bible puts it as follows, a person commits sin when he/she is drawn away of his/her own lusts and enticed (*Jas.1:14*). In the case of Adam and Eve, there was no foundation for lust because they were not sinners. But, when they entertained thoughts of disobedience and began to consider and reevaluate a course of action alien to God's Word their resistance was weakened and they fell. Satan was able to manipulate them into disobedience leading them step by step until they reached the point of no return.

The fall of Eve was a two-part process. It involved the Will of man and the Will of the flesh. The will of man was compromised and the will of the flesh was cooperative. When both of these wills fell under the control of the serpent, the deed was done.

But while the fall represented the failure of the first Adam, it opened the door for bringing in the Second Adam the Lord Jesus Christ. He is referred to as "*a quickening spirit*" (*1 Cor.15:45-47*). His foundations are spiritual; He is the God of heaven. But, He entered the natural world in a body of flesh, a natural body. In this way He was well able to be "*the Lamb of God, which taketh away the sin of the world*" (*Jn.1:29*). Whereas "*the first man is of the earth, earthy; the second man is the Lord from heaven*" (*1 Cor.15:47*).

The fall of man brought the nature of all men under sin's control "*and death by sin*" (*Roms.5:12*). Therefore, all men are dead in trespasses and sins. The eventual outcome can be averted only if salvation is found in Jesus Christ.

The fall of Adam and Eve also brought about significant change in their way of life as well. They had lost the unique qualities, which were characteristic of a man and a woman in fellowship with God. Because of this loss they experienced shame, fear, and other limitations.

Death and decay became the order of the day in God's world. The perfect natural man and the perfect natural woman had fallen. Now Eden became a desolate forsaken place overgrown with thorns. The ground no longer yielded its fruit spontaneously. All of nature suffered. What remained of Eden was likely destroyed at the time of the universal flood. The destructiveness of the fall was complete in its primary phase. Henceforth, God Himself had to become man in order to reverse the trend. But there are at least two primary consequences of the usurping of the authority of God. Both are the foundations upon which human fantasies continue to masquerade as freedom indeed.

1. *Rise of the Will of the Flesh*

When Adam fell, the nature of man was fully compromised. Not long after his death, the scriptures say, *"God saw that the wickedness of man was great in the earth and that every imagination of the thoughts of his heart was only evil continually"* (Gen.6:5). All of man's avenues of thought and communication had come under sin's control. Both the will of the flesh and the will of man became compromised. Man's freedom of choice is influenced by the will of the flesh. Therefore, it does not reflect any real freedom but rather man's bondage to sin.

There can be no doubt that after Adam and Eve had sinned, their "eyes were opened" to a knowledge of good and evil (Gen.3:7). They must have soon recognized that right and wrong, good and evil are determined by God. Therefore, even from their vantage point many things, which previously seemed, as good to them became evil. Looking at themselves through the eyes of fallen man, all of their personal actions became modified.

Outside of Eden and separated from God Adam and Eve no longer carried the halo of God's righteousness. The fall had brought about a complete change and reversal of the natural order. A life that was driven by spiritual impulses was now guided by the desires of the flesh. As it was when they discovered their nakedness the shock of sin may have opened up to them a world that was entirely new.

As sin began to take its toll, it is likely that the lives of Adam and Eve became more degenerate. Man's struggle for daily sustenance had also begun. The world around became a hostile place. The will of the flesh began to predominate in all things. Even within the lifetimes of Adam and Eve, violence began to fill the land and polygamy became acceptable. It did not take long for the fleshly desires of the hearts of men to overpower the will to please God. Even in their own household Cain, the firstborn of Adam, became completely alienated from the will of God.

Sin had moved Adam and Eve from a state of dependence on God to reliance on themselves. God no longer provided fully for their daily needs. Their struggle for survival had begun. But a whole New World was developing around them. Men and women continued to marry but immoral living was much more in evidence. The alienation of men from God and from His ways was building up to the place of universal rebellion.

But the Spirit of God continued to strive with men. Even as from the beginning when God had provided coats of skin for Adam and Eve (*Gen.3:21*). There can be no doubt that some men continued to offer sacrifice to God. In time, men like Enoch a preacher of righteousness appeared on the scene. But the power of sin and alienation that is the will of the flesh stressed out men's resistance and temporarily overpowered the grace of God. There is no evidence that the life of Adam exerted an influence for good over the quality of life that men live. The will of the flesh had risen to the place of primary influence among men. This was one of the fantasies that men thought of as the foundation of real freedom.

2. *Mistaking Darkness for Light*

The voice of God in Eden had grown inaudible or silent. The man and woman who were illuminated by God had been cast out of His presence. Because of the usurpation of God's authority men came to love darkness rather than light. Also, because the natural movement of man was towards evil continually he began to think of darkness as light. What seems to be light in the lives of natural man was really darkness continually.

The men and women being born after the fall were likely receiving mixed signals from Adam and Eve. Because of sin, they may not always have been faithful to the will of God. At any rate, the Bible says that when sin entered the world death took control (*Roms.5:12*). As the world was ushered into a period of darkness, so now there was need for light, the true Light.

Therefore, God made provision for all men coming into the world to have access to the true light. It now *"lighteth every man that cometh into the world"* (*Jn.1:9*). Without it sin would have established a barrier that blocked out access to God entirely. Even so, no man can come to the light of God's grace on his own accord. It was necessary for God to make provision to enable all men to come to know Him. The true light serves that purpose.

God also put the principle of sacrifice in place. This was the means of atonement providing a temporary reprieve for the sinner and a window for fellowship with God. This principle was renewed with Noah and his sons after the Flood (*Gen.8:20*). God gave to man new beginnings.

But, God also required a more complete sacrifice, one that was permanent and sufficient. Ultimately, it was He who became available to all men as the Sin-Bearer and door of access to the Father. In the fullness of time, God sent His Son. So great is His Light that the darkness around cannot put it out (*Jn.1:5*). By His death, burial, and resurrection the Lord Jesus Christ completely paid the price for the sin of man (*Heb.1:3*). He is the Savior, by Him all men may have peace with God (*Jn.16:33, Eph.2:14*). The door is open to provide the way by which men may return to genuine Freedom in fellowship with God.

God had endowed man with the capacity for choice. Thus, Adam and Eve were able to make choices that were separate and independent of each other. Because of this, Adam and Eve were given alternatives to obedience and alternatives to disobedience. But having chosen, man was powerless to change the consequences of his choice. Thus, when Adam and Eve rejected the choice of obedience, disobedience was their spontaneous choice. They had moved from genuine freedom to fantasy. Eve had moved away from her Freedom in Eden to a world of Fantasy. But the Father had ordained that the seed of the woman would give to all men access again to God's Freedom.

Summary

God's created world, functions within the framework of laws. The Laws of God govern all of life. When these laws are violated, there is disorder and chaos. But God made man with a free will capable of making choices even when His will is compromised. When man violated God's primary Law of life wrong was perceived as right. As it is in all of the natural world, so it was when Adam and Eve disobeyed. They fell into the range of the jurisdiction of death.

A review of the steps that led up to the fall of man reveals that an evil force had motivated him to turn away from a life of obedience. Satan had impersonated the serpent and had become the instrument in tempting man to turn away from the laws of God and live by his own personal standards. All was well in Eden with Adam and Eve before the serpent came along. But once they were drawn into communication with him, the door of spontaneous access to God became less attractive.

By nature, the serpent was wily. It was not difficult for him to draw attention to himself. But, the power of Satan at work within the serpent was sufficient to neutralize Eve's resistance. It is readily acknowledged that the archangel Lucifer commonly referred to, as Satan was the anointed cherub who himself had previously walked about in Eden (*Eze.28:13, 14*). On the other hand, God had made man "*a little lower than the angels*" (*Ps.8:5*). Therefore, in his own strength man would be no match for Satan.

Under the pressure of Satan's assault, the boundaries for living that God had created for man were brushed aside. The desires of the flesh had taken control. Eve had become so enamoured by the promises of the serpent that she momentarily placed a lower value on the promises of God. Step by step, the serpent had led the way, creating doubt and shaking her confidence in the promises of God. Before long, the alternatives he offered seemed in harmony with her own innate desires. In addition, he had convinced her that death was not really a serious consideration. He had even said that she would not die at all (*Gen.3:4*). Eventually, she came to the place where her passions were aroused and she saw the tree that was forbidden from a different perspective. At that point, her fall was inevitable.

It would seem that God has granted both to men and angels a measure of freedom of choice. God made no provision for the Repentance of Angels (*Jude 6*), but for man, made in His image, God has put an alternative plan in place. As a first step in that plan the scriptures say that God went after Adam and Eve seeking them out after their fall (*Gen.3:8,9*). God then made for them "*coats of skins and clothed them*" (*Gen.3:21*). By these steps, the lines of communication between God and man were partially reopened. Eventually, Eve's conquering seed came to the rescue, even Jesus Christ.

The temptation and fall had its effects on both Adam and Eve. But, the process of the temptation had made of Eve a different woman. The desires of her flesh would now always transcend the desires of the spirit. Her mindset was changed. The actual eating of the fruit changed her emotions and overpowered all other considerations. She saw all things in a completely different light. She saw God differently and from her perspective, Adam became a different person too. The elements of desire took full possession of her decisions. It became natural for her to secure her husband's involvement in the fall.

In some respects both Adam and Eve may have failed each other. But, it is likely that before the fall there was no sensuous bond between them. He had no compulsions to give direction to Eve before she had fallen. In the case of Eve however, she had already fallen when she turned to influence him to walk in her direction. In all respects, the Divine order of God was compromised. Therefore, the man and woman entered a period of disorder. Whereas the laws of God had established order, violations of those laws had resulted in chaos.

The fall of man brought evil into the world. Satan had become a player in the affairs of men. In all matters, he would strive to replace the authority of God and distort the nature of the authority of man. In order to deal with this new power God made changes in the duties of Adam and Eve. He added two new dimensions to Eve's relationship with her husband. The first was *"thy desire shall be to thy husband."* The next was *"and he shall rule over thee"* (*Gen.3:16*). These new conditions involved hardships, which both would find difficult to overcome except with the help of God. But, the heart of man had become evil. Sin had alienated him from God and caused him to be in a state of rebellion. God's Divine order with respect to men and women was completely compromised. Eve was a changed woman now empowered with the capacity to turn the hearts of men around. The woman had turned God's world into a place where men's fantasies are often paraded as freedom.

Dr. Roderick Loney

67

The Legacy of Eve

Adam and Eve, Reflections

Not once, but many times, or often
Adam may to Eve have spoken
Of the tree that God had said
If you eat, you will be dead

"How could that be?" Eve may have thought
"Could such a fruit be good for naught?
Could it thus hide beneath its bark?
The kiss of death the final mark?"

It made no sense to Eve at least
That such a fruit could be a _beast_
Hiding beneath its sweet perfume
The kiss of death pathway to doom

Was Eve a-sulking on the side?
Thinking, the thoughts she tried to hide?
If so, the wily Serpent thought
She may be easy to be _bought_

By asking her about the tree
And God's command of what should be
Serpent talk quite soon revealed
How much power she could wield

How wonderful and wise she thought?
Could it be for _her good_ he sought
The words he spoke sounded so sure
Could she indeed know _So Much More_?

Irreligious though the thought
Deceived she was and all for naught

Dr. Roderick Loney

Should she now let her Adam know
God really had not said it so?

Perhaps just what the serpent said
Could place them so much more ahead
But could she from her husband hide
Just what she wanted to decide?

She made her choice she ate the fruit
Then came to Adam *looking cute*
She told him too in gentle words
That he should eat not only birds

So Adam thought Eve he *MUST* please
He could not leave her, like a breeze
So he decided he would take
Of that same fruit, not her forsake!

He looked again, how could it be
Is Eve all naked, did I see?
And she to him then did reply
"Dear Adam, *Will we surely Die?*"

"That must not be," he thought, but then,
Slick serpent slipped into his den
Nowhere they found him though they looked
He fled the scene by hook and crook

Adam did cry, and Eve lament,
That God's clear Word they both had bent
"Let's hide from God" this was the thought
Perhaps a way out could be sought

So with the fig leaves they were covered
Filled with shame and things that bothered

The Legacy of Eve

Then behind the bushes they
Concealed themselves in every way

Filled now with terror, how much they trembled
All around them the ground had rumbled
God was carrying out His rounds
As He went strolling through the grounds

When He drew near, they knew for certain
That soon He would be at their curtain
Bushes could not hide from Him
All the noise and all that din

Everywhere in Eden fair
Noise and noise now filled the air
All of nature in alarm
Things could not be a state of calm

Suddenly, there was the Word
God was calling, and Adam heard
For God had said "where are you hiding
Are you no more in me abiding?"

Adam cried out "not *Me* Lord *She*
Of the fruit Eve gave to me"
And in my weakness I gave way
Fearing to lose her for "a day"

Eve also spoke chiming right in
How slick the serpent made her sin
And how in fact she turned away
Hoping for a better day

Then God again looked all around

Dr. Roderick Loney

And found old "Slick" inside the ground
To him He said "dust shalt thou eat"
Slide on thy belly as is fitting and meet

But here the story does not end
For God had surely lost His friend
Consigned to death was he and she
No longer in God's company

And soon in time they saw no gain
In introducing sin and shame
Out of the Garden they must go
To face a world of weal and woe

The destiny of man to be
To Hell for all eternity
But then, the blessed Savior came
To cover Sin and take the Blame

CHAPTER 3
Contesting the restraints of One-fleshing

The prevailing mood in the days of Noah was that *"the sons of God saw the daughters of men that they were fair and they took them wives all which they chose"* (*Gen.6:2*). It would seem that the images projected by the women of that day clearly reflected the inducement of Eve towards Adam in Eden. Choosing the woman seemed to be more significant for man than obeying God. Female seductiveness seems to have turned aside even the sons of God. The laws of God concerning one fleshing were flagrantly cast aside. What seems to be the woman's perspective exercised more effective control of human behavior and put in place a new tone of morality.

The Bible adds that there was violence in the land as well. It is not clear whether such violence was an outgrowth of sexual indiscretion. But the Bible also says, *"the wickedness of man was great in the earth"* (*Gen. 6:5*). All things considered, the stage was set for God's Divine intervention. Therefore God raised up Noah, a preacher of righteousness. He followed in the footsteps of Enoch his foreparent who also "walked with God."

The social climate significantly affected the lives of men on earth in their relationships with God. Violation of the laws of one fleshing altered the conditions of living. During these earlier times, the influence of women was more subtle. The laws of the land still assigned men to the primary place in all relationships. But the influence of the daughters of Eve moved all things into a changing social mode. Among the daughters of Eve, discontent was stirring. Step by step, women began to find ways to circumvent oppressive man-made laws.

That, *"the sons of God saw the daughters of men that they were fair"* (*Gen 6:2*) gives a hint that steps were being taken by women to increase

73

their sensuous attractiveness. Isaiah makes reference to a similar condition as he described the new look of the daughters of Zion. In the words of the prophet, they had begun to *"walk with stretched forth necks and wanton eyes walking and mincing as they go and making a tinkling with their feet"* (*Isaiah 3:16ff*). Maybe these were echoes of the seduction of Eve, which led Adam to eat of the fruit.

There can be no doubt that the primary modus of Eve had set a precedent for women. One needs to be reminded that Eve had come to the place where, *"she saw that the tree was good for food that it was pleasant to the eyes"* (*Gen. 3:6*). She was determined that Adam should see it her way. Eve herself went beyond the visible pleasantness of sin to find that the tree was, *"desirable to make one wise"* (*Gen. 3:6*). All this was contrary to God's order of things.

The strength of "desire" continued to be the trademark of the woman. In this instance, the desire of the woman had been the instrument for bringing sin into the world. The power of the woman's desire seemed unstoppable. It is quite likely that because of this condition God moved to strengthen the authority of the man to have the rule over the woman. For God had said to the woman, *"your desire shall be for your husband and he shall rule over thee"* (*Gen. 3:16*). The desire of the woman that was contrary to the Word of God had become sin.

Human desire continues to be an obstacle to faith. As the context of life outside of the garden became more stressful, men and women kept on reaching out to make adjustments. All men felt free to follow the devices and desires of their own hearts. God was not at all in their thoughts. The early exploits of men after the fall reflect the direction in which the thoughts of men were leading them. Polygamy and violence were not unusual. Even the adjustments made in the rules of living for the man and woman seemed to have had limited salutary effects.

The scriptures summarized the state of affairs for all men even as early as the days of Noah. Remember the theme of those days was that, *"the wickedness of man was great in the earth, and...every intent of the thoughts of his heart was only evil continually"* (*Gen.6:5*). To add to that, the population explosion and enhancement of the female image contributed to the breakdown of socio-moral restraints. The desires of men's hearts had become sin; they tested the moral and spiritual restraints of one-fleshing in significant ways.

Enhancing the Physical Image

The sons of Cain and Lamech in particular boasted of having more than one wife. By the time of Noah, polygamy had become an accepted way of life. The Post-Adamic woman had learned to enhance her attractiveness. The process continued unchecked from one generation to the next even in situations where women were required by law to be veiled in public. A review of that practice today finds virtue and chastity in attire as outmoded and unfashionable. The daughters of Eve walk the streets of modern cities almost naked or leaving very little to the imagination.

The Lord Jesus Himself made the comparison when He said, *"as it was in the days of Noah so shall it be also in the days of the Son of man"* (*Lk.17:26*).

Enoch also, a preacher of righteousness commented on the practice of *"having men's persons in admiration"* (*Jude 16*). Over and over again, reference was made to the "ungodly" of his day. It is important to note also that *"the sons of God"* mentioned here have no reference to angelic beings, as some would suggest. The testimony of Enoch and the preaching Noah were addressed to sinful men. It was intended for the sons of Adam, to provide deliverance for them from the waters of the Flood.

In those days, men and women continued to marry and to be given in marriage. But the quality of man's life on earth had changed. Somehow, it seems that women continued to maintain the "pulling power" of Eve in drawing men away from loyalty to God. In some respects, she had redefined the role of women in their relationships with men.

The Bible describes an event in the life of Abraham when he was about to sojourn into Egypt. It highlights the issue. He said to his wife Sarah, *"I know that thou art a fair woman to look upon"* (*Gen.12:11*). He reasoned that Pharaoh will hear about her, want her to be his wife, and will kill him to get her if necessary. Therefore, Abraham asked his wife to say that she was his sister (*Gen.12:9-13*). Abraham's initial assessment was quite correct. The Egyptians *"beheld the woman that she was very fair...the woman was taken into Pharaoh's house"* (Abraham's nephew) (*Gen.12:14, 15*).

Sexual promiscuity had become widespread and sexual aberrations with them. Men became sexually involved with other men also. The event around the destruction of Sodom and Gomorrah presents a classic case involving male visitors at the home of Lot (*Gen.19:1ff*).

These are the trends that had begun to refashion relationships between men and women. The Bible records significant changes in public behavior with respect to one-fleshing. Divorce and multiple female partners in marriage became acceptable and accommodated by law even in Israel. Jacob, the father of the twelve tribes of the nation had two wives. The laws of Ur-of-the-Chaldees made allowances for Concubinage. All of the Kings of Israel had concubines and King Solomon is said to have had one thousand wives. The Lord Jesus Himself commented upon the state of affairs, saying that God allowed Moses to write laws on this issue because of the hardness of man's hearts (*Matt.19:8ff*).

The process continues today. There is hardly any society in which allowances are not made to legalize promiscuous behavior. Much of public advertising is tuned to the enhanced sex appeal of women. The restraints of the laws of one-fleshing as ordained by God receive little public acceptance even in many places where God is worshipped. The enhanced female image has become the trademark for selling many products.

Manipulating Male Authority

Rebekah became the wife of Isaac under all of the traditional arrangements that were consistent with the times in which they lived. Abraham did not wish to take a wife for his son *"from the daughters of the Canaanites"* among whom he lived (*Gen.24:3*). Therefore, he requested that his steward Eliezer of Damascus choose a woman from among his kindred.

In due course Abraham's steward returned to the homeland. There he met Rebekah almost as an answer to prayer. She was the granddaughter of Nahor the brother of Abraham. Arrangements were made with her parents and she consented to go with him to become the wife of Isaac.

At her first meeting with Isaac Rebekah had *"dismounted from her camel...took a veil and covered herself"* (*Gen.24:64-65*). Subsequently, Isaac *"brought her into his mother Sarah's tent; and he took Rebekah and she became his wife"* (*Gen.24:67*). She demonstrated all of the virtues of a wife who was the help meet for her husband even as Sarai.

But, before long, it became evident that Rebekah experienced difficulty in submitting to the authority of her husband on some issues. When their sons Jacob and Esau were grown, Rebekah conceived a plan to insure that her favorite son Jacob received the Blessing instead of Esau. That the birthright should go to the younger was God's promise. But the plans of God could have gone forward without Rebekah's intervention. However, she became anxious and manipulated the truth for the expressed purpose of deceiving her husband.

Rebekah had arranged for her son Jacob to disguise himself as his brother Esau. She prepared a meal for her husband, as Esau would have done it.

Next, she briefed Jacob on the manner in which he should proceed to tell lies to his father. In the event that anything went wrong, Rebekah had said to Jacob, *"let your curse be on me"* (*Gen.27:13*). She had completely put aside any thought of submitting to her husband on an issue that meant so much to her. The Bible bears record of similar issues that began to characterize the relationships between women and men.

Rachel also the daughter of Laban had claimed "feminine privilege" as a means of thwarting her father's attempt to find his Teraphim. But it was hidden under her seat. Later on, she expressed her own frustration with her sister Leah who continued to be fertile while she remained barren. In an outburst of rage Rachel demanded of her husband Jacob, *"give me children or else I die"* (*Gen.30:1*).

The Bible described in some detail the case of Rahab the harlot and the steps that she took to protect the spies whom Joshua had sent to spy out the land. The King of Jericho had heard of it and sent messengers to Rahab's home. But, Rahab was able to provide protection for the spies and convince the messengers to seek for them elsewhere.

Ruth also the daughter-in-law of Naomi was able to influence Boaz to look with favor upon her. Under the coaching of her mother-in-law, he became fired-up to seek her interest. Eventually, Boaz married Ruth (*Ruth 4:13*). At a critical juncture along the way, Naomi had advised Ruth to

> *"Wash thyself therefore, and anoint thee, and put thy raiment upon thee, and get thee down to the floor; but make not thyself known unto the man, until he shall have done eating and drinking. And it shall be, when he lieth down, that thou shalt mark the place where he shall lie, and thou shalt go in, and uncover his feet, and lay thee down; and he will tell thee what thou shalt do"* (*Ruth 3:3,4*).

As a result of this action Boaz replied *"and now my daughter, fear not: I will do to thee all that thou requirest"* (*Ruth 3:11*).

The roster of female manipulation included Esther queen of Persia. She engineered a scheme to destroy the wicked plot of Haman to murder the Jews. For Haman had said to the king *"if it please the king let it be written that they may be destroyed: and I will pay ten thousand talents of silver to the hands of those that have the charge of the business"* (*Est.3:9*). As a result of this scheme *"letters were sent by posts into all the kings provinces, to destroy, to kill, and to cause to perish, all Jews, both young and old, little children and women, in one day"* (*Est.3:13*).

But on the thirteenth day of the twelfth month, the entire situation was reversed. Queen Esther was able to design her own plan for turning the anger of the King against Haman. Therefore, the gallows, which Haman had built for another he himself, was hanged upon it (*Est.7:10*). The feast of Purim became a day of rejoicing for Jews rather than a time of grief. As a general rule, it would seem that impulses deep within the hearts of men and women were driving them in directions that were contrary to the moral laws of God.

But, the list of women who manipulated their husbands in Bible times would be incomplete without the name of Jezebel. She was the wife of Ahab King of Israel. On one occasion, the King was sulking over a matter concerning a vineyard that he desired. She took over the reins of government and abused the authority of the King with impunity.

Jezebel had said to her husband, *"Dost thou now govern the kingdom of Israel...I will give thee the vineyard of Naboth the Jezreelite"* (*1 Ki.21:7*). She then promptly sent out the letters in the King's name and sealed with the King's seal. False charges were brought against Naboth and he was killed. After all the processes were completed, Jezebel said to her husband the King, *"Arise, take possession of the vineyard of Naboth the Jezreelite which he refused to give thee for money"* (*1 Ki.21:15*).

The times of the twentieth century have witnessed the emergence of women's movements that have transformed the social order. The struggle for gender equality has become an accepted practice in most modern societies. The idea that "sameness" is the evidence of that equality is also an accepted notion. In this respect, the manipulation of male authority has achieved its objective. However, the laws of natural design still hold true that "form follows function." The body structure of men and women equip them for functions that are distinctly different. But here also the rebellion of Eve has cast aside the Divine restraints of the laws of one-fleshing.

Sharing Male Authority

The Flood was a significant turning point in man's life on planet earth. God made a new beginning. He gave to Noah a new mandate saying, *"be fruitful, and multiply, and replenish the earth"* (*Gen.9:1*). However in one respect the covenant with Noah was different. God added the words, *"the fear of you and the dread of you shall be upon every beast of the earth"* (*Gen.9:2*).

The world had become unfriendly and hostile. A wall of fear had arisen between man and beast. More than ever man would now need the abiding presence of God to guide every step of the way. God took steps to open special lines of communication with man. He instructed Noah to build *"an altar unto the Lord"* (*Gen.8:20*) for the Glory of God had departed from the earth.

Even so, sin was soon in the ascendancy again Noah himself lapsed into a period of indiscretion. He planted a vineyard, drank of the wine and was overcome. In a state of drunkenness, he lay uncovered in his tent. It seems that Cain the son of Ham had looked upon his grandfather with lustful intent. At any rate, he communicated with his father but no steps were taken to cover Noah's shame. This event led to a curse upon Canaan (*Gen.9:20ff*). The issue has been interpreted in a variety of ways. Quite often, it has been cited as a rational for elements of racial discrimination. But the emphasis in the scriptures is upon the hand of God at work in the affairs of men.

Nimrod was of Noah's hire but he rebelled against God. Changes in human language and speech at Babel drove men and women to the Four Corners of the earth. The identity of God and the nature of worship was being transformed. Different accounts of the creation sprang up along with changing perceptions of God. As nations multiplied, the knowledge of God became diffused and the roles of women became varied. However, polygamy and male dominance thrived wherever men were found.

Eventually, the plan of God for the salvation of men entered a different phase. The call of God went out to Abraham in Ur of the Chaldees. God had directed him to, *"get thee out of thy country and from thy kindred...and I will make of thee a great nation"* (*Gen.12:1, 2*). Abraham obeyed the voice of God and left Ur of the Chaldees taking with him his wife Sarai and his nephew Lot.

In the course of time, decisions had to be made concerning Abraham's heir. His wife Sarai was barren. But she agreed to have her handmaid Hagar bear children on her behalf. This matter became an issue of even greater significance when God healed Sarai of her barrenness at a later date. She gave birth to a son named Isaac and insisted that the bondwoman (Hagar) and her son Ishmael be sent away (*Gen.21: 10*). She would have no one to share the heritage with Isaac. It is this child of promise who became the husband of Rebekah as mentioned earlier in the text.

The Book of Exodus presents a summary of significant events in the process of establishing God's chosen nation. It was a period of rapid growth for the sons of Jacob. But it represented a period of significant collaboration also between men and women. Before long, the people of Israel became a significant threat to Pharaoh. He placed them in bondage. Laws were put into effect to control their growing influence. There was even a law in place to destroy all male babies at birth.

Then God raised up women of courage who carried on roles beyond the reach of men. Two were outstanding, Shiprah and Puah, Jewish midwives. At the risk of their own lives, they found ways to disobey the orders of the king. They *"feared God and did not as the king of Egypt commanded them but saved the men children alive"* (*Exo.1:17*).

The timely action of Shiprah and Puah set the stage for the coming of Moses. In due course, other courageous women joined in the struggle also. Jochebed, the mother of Moses played a significant part in the nurture of her son following the actions of the midwives. She used the reprieve to seek other alternatives to preserve his life. The Bible describes her efforts as acts of faith, saying, *"by faith Moses, when he was born, was hid three months of his parents, because they saw he was a proper child; and they were not afraid of the king's commandment"* (*Heb.11:23*).

Subsequently, Jochebed involved her daughter Miriam in the venture to preserve the life of Moses. They prepared an ark for the child and placed it in the river near to the bathing spot of Pharaoh's daughter. As it happened, she found the child and took steps to adopt him into her family. With the help of Miriam the sister of Moses, Jochebed his mother became his nurse (*Exo.2:1-10*). For Miriam herself, much more lay ahead on the journey to the Promised Land. Again and again, it seems that in every situation where the interests of women were at stake, they were willing to do whatever was necessary to advance those interests.

At a much later date, when Moses was grown, apparently Miriam did not approve of *"the Ethiopian woman whom he had married"* (*Nums.12:1*). In the misunderstanding that developed, she added the statement *"hath the Lord indeed spoken only by Moses? Hath he not spoken also by us?"* (*Num.12:2*). In this way, both Miriam and Aaron were challenging the leadership of Moses at a critical period. The scriptures record that the judgment of God fell upon them both (*Num.12:9ff*).

As Israel continued on their journey to the Promised Land there were several points along the way where the influence of women made the difference for good as well as for evil. A significant matter is described when Israel had encamped on the borders of Moab. The Moabite king Balak sought the services of Balaam (a well-known seer) to curse the armies of Israel. All of the efforts of Balaam failed. As a last resort, he suggested that the armies of Israel be compromised with Moabite women (*Rev.2:14, Jude 11*). The king of Moab sent them in among the troops. The deed was done. *"The people began to commit whoredom with the daughters of Moab"* (*Num.25:1-3*). In this way, the hearts of many were turned away from God and judgment fell upon Israel (*Num.31:16, Rev.2:14*). A plague broke out among the people.

The number of *"those that died in the plague were twenty and four thousand"* (*Num.25:9*). One event is singled out which points to the gravity of the situation. An Israelite man brought unto his brethren a *"Midianitish woman in the sight of Moses"* (*Num.25:6*). This same man took the woman into his tent and was intimately involved with her. Phinehas of the house of the priest went after them. He *"thrust both of them through, the man of Israel, and the woman through her belly. So the plague was stayed from the children of Israel"* (*Num.25:8*). The name of the woman was Cozbi, the daughter of Zur (*Num.25:15*).

The period of the Judges provided unique opportunities for interchanging roles between men and women. Of this period the Bible says that the former *"generation were gathered unto their fathers: and there arose another generation after them, which knew not the Lord"* (*Judg.2:10*). The Bible says of this time that because *"there was no king in Israel...every man did that which was right in his own eyes"* (*Judg.17:6*) that included, every woman also.

The events that led to the deliverance from Egypt and the crossing of the Red Sea were soon forgotten. God's own chosen people had turned to the worship of idols, particularly, Baal and Ashtaroth (*Judg.2:13*). In due course, God raised up Judges to bring a measure of order to daily living. But these judges were both men and women. An outstanding woman named Deborah, the wife of Lapidoth was among the Judges of Israel. She was called a "prophetess" (*Judg.4:4*), in much the same way as Miriam (*Exo.15:20*) or Huldah (*2 Ki. 22:14*). However, unlike many of the prophets of the Old Testament these prophetesses in many respects served somewhat as Seers.

During the period of the Judges, the rule of Divine authority had come full circle. Women became very active in taking the initiatives normally associated with men. In a general sense, as it was with many of the judges of that period, there was little evidence of God's Divine intervention at work. The name Deborah became outstanding in Israel because of the initiatives she took in assisting Barak in a critical battle. He had said to her, "*if thou wilt go with me, then I will go; but if thou wilt not go with me, then I will not go. And she said I will surely go with thee*" (*Judg.4:8, 9*). At any rate, it was Deborah who initiated the victory over the army of Sisera (*Judg.4:14*).

A woman named Delilah also played a pivotal role in the life of Samson one of the judges of Israel. She accomplished what the armies of the Philistines were unable to do. The man Samson was feared for his unusual strength. He had the reputation of having killed a young lion with his bare hands (*Judg.14:6*). Also, on one occasion, he "*took the doors of the gate of the city and the two posts and went away with them*" (*Judg.16:3*). But Delilah used her feminine charm to deceive Samson and facilitate his capture by the Philistines (*Judg.16:5-17*).

Ruth the Moabitess was another outstanding person who became well known as a virtuous woman in Israel (*Ruth 3:11*). She was the daughter-in-law of Naomi and had identified herself with the God of Israel. Under normal terms of the Mosaic Law "*an Ammonite or Moabite shall not enter into the congregation of the Lord even to their tenth generation shall they not enter into the congregation of the Lord forever*"

(*Deut.23:3*). But Ruth became an exception. She had deliberately turned away from her people to serve the living God. Subsequently, God rewarded her faith; she became the wife of Boaz, and gave birth to a son whose name was Obed. Now Obed was the father of Jesse, the father of David (*Ruth 4:16, 17*).

The story of Ruth is well known. By all accounts, she was of gentle disposition. But, this gentle virtuous woman under the guidance of Naomi had learned how to manipulate Boaz and work with him to serve her best interests. The principle of one-fleshing was being modified in ways that were changing God's initial design.

There were times too when standing in for the man simply meant influencing him to do that which the woman desired. The record of the scriptures does not provide much detail concerning overt struggles of women for equal status with men. But, it does examine a wide range of instances in which women had both succeeded where men had failed and overruled the man's choice when it was unfavorable. The process of sharing male authority became an integral part of daily life in many communities.

Redefining the Help Meet

When God created the woman, He had provided for the man a help that was meet for him (*Gen.2:18*). But the fall of man significantly altered man's nature and the natural world in which he lived. In anticipation of the needs of fallen men and women, God redefined the rules of living for both the man and the woman. Even so, the power of sin continued to make inroads. God raised up preachers of righteousness and brought in severe judgments. But man's sex drives overrode all other primary interests. Polygamy was out of control. It had a sustained impact on men of every generation. In order to facilitate this process laws were put in place for divorce as well. The primary role of the helpmeet was redefined. Our Lord Jesus in a comment in the New Testament reminded the Jews that Moses had made concessions because of the hardness of men's hearts (*Matt.19:8*).

During the period of the Judges, mention was made of a woman named Hannah. She was described as one of two wives of a man named Elkanah. Yet she became the mother of Samuel a primary prophet in Israel. God had given to Hannah a Divine reprieve and granted her request for a son who was in turn given back to God. Had the laws of God changed with respect to the marriage bond? The answer is "No." But the scriptures say that, "hardness of heart" had taken place and fallen men lost the capacity for primary obedience.

The practice of polygamy had become an acceptable "*modus operandi*" even for the children of Israel. In the Book of Leviticus, laws were introduced to govern the relationships between men and women including one who was not the primary wife. But despite the relaxation of the law, violations continued. The scriptures indicate that even the sons of Eli, who were priests themselves, made it a habit to "*lay with the women that assembled at the door of the tabernacle of the congregation*" (*1 Sam.2:22*).

At a much later date in the history of the nation of Israel an occasion arose in which it was noted that, "*all the chief of the priests, and the people, transgressed very much after all the abominations of the heathen; and polluted the house of the Lord...till there was no remedy*" (*2 Chro.36:14-16*). Corruption and sexual immorality continued even after Israel had returned from Babylonian captivity. The prophet Ezra sounded a note of alarm when it was determined that "*the holy seed have mingled themselves with the people of those lands*" (*Ezra 9:2*). Therefore, he led the people to covenant with God "*to put away all the wives, and such as are born of them, according to the counsel of the Lord*" (*Ezra 10:3*).

The prophet Nehemiah too expressed his concern for the *stumblings* of his people. It was recorded that Tobiah (one of the chief adversaries of the Jews) was son-in-law of Shechaniah a noble of Judah. Further, that Tobiah's son had taken to wife the daughter of Meshullam [another noble of Judah] (*Neh.6:17ff*). The "*Jews that had married wives of Ashdod, of Ammon, and of Moab*" (*Neh.13:23ff*), were reminded of the sins that befell King Solomon because of his "*outlandish women*" (*Neh.13:26*).

In a continuing survey of the Bible record, God had said to the prophet Hosea, "*Go take unto thee a wife of whoredoms*" (*Hos.1:2*). Therefore, Hosea married Gomer the daughter of Diblain (*Hos.1:3*). The assignment given to Hosea was unique. Nonetheless, God used this example to illustrate the attitude of Israel towards Jehovah Himself. But, the emphasis here was upon Gomer. The illustration served to call attention to the spiritual adultery of the nation of Israel.

By the time of the coming of Jesus of Nazareth traditions concerning marriage had been fixed even in Israel. The laws established by Moses served as guidelines for all relationships between men and women. But, the basic teachings of the Word of God with respect to the principle of one-fleshing were ignored.

A wide range of sexual configurations were in place. A story was told in the Book of Judges concerning a Levite and his concubine (*Jud.19:1ff*). It highlighted also the widespread practice of sodomy that seemed to have been well established since the days of Lot.

By the time of the Judges, relationships between men and women were altered. These changed attitudes began to make a significant impact upon the terms and conditions of life in the society as a whole. In the face of what has become a growing apostasy it is necessary to review again the specific Laws of God with respect to these matters. Special attention will be paid to "multiplying wives" and "putting away wives."

1. *Multiplying Wives:*

God had created the woman to be appealing to the man so that he would be drawn towards her. Literally, she was designed to be the help that was meet for his every need. In this way the man would be driven by an inner sense of urgency to fulfill God's command to *"be fruitful and multiply"* (Gen.1:28). Thus, when Adam beheld Eve for the first time, he found her to be appealing. There was a sense of elation when he cried out *"this is now bone of my bones and flesh of my flesh"* (Gen.2:23). So strong was the "pull" of Eve that it overruled his passions.

In the epistles of Paul, a statement is made concerning the natural use of the woman and of the man. As God intended it, it is quite natural for men to be drawn towards women, and women to be drawn towards men. But, this natural attraction was to be subject to God's Law. In due course, a man and a woman would find that one to whom they would become bound in a lifelong relationship. But, when man fell there was a departure from God's natural order. Man's natural impulses went out of control. The whole nature of man came under the powers of death. The attitudes and desires of men were also transformed.

Thus, the scriptures say,

> *"For even their women did change the natural use into that which is against nature: and likewise also the men, leaving the natural use of the woman, burned in their lust one toward another; men with men working that which is unseemly"* (Roms.1:26, 27).

Sexual attraction is a natural impulse, but between members of the same sex it is unnatural.

By all accounts, the universal flood in the days of Noah was God's primary instrument for purging out sin in that generation. Methuselah was about 969 years old and Adam had already passed away. The Bible specifically describes the flood as a response to the violations of the laws of life. *"The sons of God saw the daughters of men that they were fair; and took them wives of all which they chose"* (Gen.6:2).

The Bible commented that, *"the Lord saw that the wickedness of man was great in the earth."* God also saw that *"every imagination of the thoughts of his heart was only evil continually"* (Gen.6:5). The promiscuity of men had reached the Divine flash-point of disobedience. The preaching of Enoch, [he *"walked with God"* (Gen.5:24)] seems to have had little sustaining impact even upon the sons of God. They too had become polygamous and were multiplying wives.

Only, *"Noah found grace in the eyes of the Lord"* (Gen.6:8). He was a unique man, out of step with the perversity of his day and diligent to obey the Word of God. He preached a message of repentance and salvation. It was addressed to the sons of men even those who were called "sons of God." There is nothing to indicate that the integrity of the scriptures was breached at any point. Noah did not bring a message of hope to angels; it was tuned to the hearts of men. It is obvious that the Flood would have had no impact upon the lives of "angels."

The practice of multiplying wives was and continues to be an affront to God. It abuses the sanctified process of sex and procreation that were ordained by God. God's purpose was that man would *"be fruitful, and multiply and replenish the earth"* (Gen.1:28). Polygamy shifts the emphasis from pleasing God to pleasing self, from the Divine purpose to sensual pleasure as an end in itself. The entire principle of one-fleshing is abused when it is limited simply to bonding in the flesh. In the annals of the history of men, sexual perversion has often become a weathervane for Divine judgment.

After the Flood, man was given the opportunity for a new beginning. God again had said, *"be fruitful and multiply and replenish the earth"* (Gen.9:1). Even so, it was not long before the hearts of men were turned away from God. With the rise of Nimrod and the move to rebel against

God, polygamy was sure to be a recurring condition. Remember what the Bible says of Nimrod, that he *"began to be a mighty one in the earth. He was a mighty hunter before the Lord"* (Gen.10:8, 9). Nimrod hunted for the hearts and loyalties of men. His interest was purely secular and self-centered. Sexual sins would usually thrive in such a setting.

After some time Abram came along. The Code may have served as a guide to Sarai Abram's wife when she decided to bear children by her handmaid Hagar. Even Laban the father of Leah and Rachel seems to have been guided by recommendations in that same Code of Hammurabi. He had said to Jacob *"it must not be so done in our country to give the younger before the firstborn"* (Gen.29:26). Therefore, he had no scruples in giving to Jacob both of his daughters as wives.

Later on, among the Hebrews the laws concerning Levirate marriage were put in place. By this means, provision was made for the right of inheritance. But, there are conditions under which that principle itself may have been contrary to the law of one-fleshing. The observation of the Lord Jesus Christ many years later should be repeated. He noted that Moses had made allowances in the law *"because of the hardness of your hearts"* (Matt.19:8). However, He continued, *"that he which made them at the beginning made them male and female...wherefore they are no more twain, but one flesh"* (Matt.19:4-6).

Polygamy or the multiplying of wives was entrenched in Israel. Today it manifests itself among most peoples everywhere. In many societies, laws are designed to accommodate the interests of common-law wives and concubines of every sort. Especially among those of the Moslem faith, the right to maintain a harem is an accepted practice. There is no such adjustment in God's law of one fleshing. The practice of multiplying wives has redefined sexual roles.

2. *Putting Away Wives:*

The matter of putting away a wife has often been a source of controversy in many societies. This process became an issue of increasing significance as men continued to multiply upon the face of the earth and Concubinage became the accepted way. But the habits and attitudes of men do not alter Divine intent. Among the children of Israel, a woman who was put away carried a negative stigma. A priest could not "*take a wife who is a harlot or a defiled woman, nor shall they take a woman divorced from her husband for the priest is holy to his God*" (*Lev.21:7*). The Lord Jesus had reminded the Pharisees of this matter.

By way of a summary to the discussion the Lord continued saying, of a married couple that, "*they are no more twain, but one flesh. What therefore God hath joined together, let not man put asunder*" (*Matt.19:5, 6*). He went further to add that "*whosoever shall put away his wife, except it be for fornication, and shall marry another, committeth adultery: and whoso marrieth her which is put away doth commit adultery*" (*Matt.19:9*).

The apostle Paul commented that,

> "*The woman which hath an husband is bound by the law to her husband so long as he liveth; but if the husband be dead she is loosed from the law of her husband. So then if while her husband liveth she be married to another man she shall be called an adulteress*" (*Roms.7:2, 3*).

God requires a person to be faithful to the marriage vow. The Bible also says "*let not the wife depart from her husband: but and if she depart, let her remain unmarried, or be reconciled to her husband: and let not the husband put away his wife*" (*1 Cor.7:10, 11*).

The message of the scriptures is clear. As it applies to bishops or church officers, the observation of the Apostle Paul to Timothy, states that "*a bishop then must be blameless, a husband of one wife*" (*1 Tim.3:2*).

Literally, the term translated "*one wife*" properly interpreted refers to "one and the same woman." Therefore it may be concluded, that church leaders are expected to observe a more rigid code of behavior. It is unlikely that remarriage is allowed to them even in the instance of the death of a spouse.

The terms and conditions set forth by Moses had declared that a man could give his wife a bill of divorcement if "*she find no favor in his eyes, because he hath found some uncleanness in her*" (*Deut.24:1*). In such cases, the woman would be free to remarry (*Deut.24:2*). However, if the wife was a woman taken from among the captives, the process of separation was simple. In summary, it said that, "*If thou have no delight in her, then thou shalt let her go whither she will*" (*Deut.21:14*). In the instances where wives were taken from among idol-worshipping Gentile women, a similar process seems to have been followed.

Despite all of the violations of the Law of God by men, Mosaic Law often held women to a higher standard. In the event that a woman was found to have lost her virginity before marriage, the penalty was harsh. "*The men of her city shall stone her with stones that she die: because she had wrought folly in Israel, to play the whore in her father's house*" (*Deut.22:21*). There was no test of male virginity and for the woman seeking a divorce; the process was even far more complex.

To put away one's wife with impunity is not enshrined in the Word of God. Violation of the vows of marriage through separation or divorce gives rise to insurmountable problems in the lives of children and undermines the moral foundations of a society. It emphasizes the desires of the heart of fallen men and should not be an option among those who uphold the standards set forth in the Word of God.

However it may be defined, the reference to one-fleshing renders all other arrangements null and void. Without regard to their social or religious orientations, neither the man nor the woman is free to remarry except at the death of the spouse. It needs to be repeated that Moses was responding to the *hardness of heart* of the people when he set forth terms and conditions for divorce. The foundations of God's Divine marriage principle remain unchanged.

The principle of one-fleshing as ordained by God brings dignity to the lives of the man and the woman who are joined together in marriage. Human alternatives to the law of God redefine the man and the woman whom God has created in His Image. Both tend to become "disposable baggage" who are only valuable when they serve the needs of the other. The changing roles of men and women have continued to set the stage for confusion concerning the terms of equality for men and women. The special needs of the man and the woman as God has created them have all but disappeared as social restraints also fall away. New values, new orientation, and a new dynamic now exist. But these cannot meet the deep passionate needs within the hearts of men who developed different ways to resist the restraints of one-fleshing.

Summary

All the evidence reveals that as far back as the history of man can be documented "Homo sapiens" continues as God has created him. Basic man made in the Image of God has not evolved. But there have been changes in the nature of man because of sin. At the time of the fall, God (the Creator) retuned the lives of Adam and Eve to accommodate death. He reinforced the distinctions between the duties of the man and the duties of the woman stressing the differences in sexual roles. But almost immediately, men began to violate these distinctions and reinterpret sexual functions.

The fall of man significantly distorted the human perspective. Progressively, sex roles were reinterpreted in terms of perceived needs. New guidelines emerged in the relationships between men and women. The needs of the flesh progressively over-powered the needs of the human spirit. They became the driving forces, which moved man farther away from God. Many women learned how to manipulate men and male sexual appetites found little satisfaction in the one fleshing standard designed by God.

Intimate relationships between men and women changed significantly. In some respects, women became more involved in the affairs of state. But the spread of polygamy changed forever the significance of the bond of one fleshing. All of life underwent change. The population explosion along with the early development of urban centers brought men together in ways that tested the very foundations of morality.

The social and/or moral implications of non-binding sexual relationships began to create havoc within the society of men. The foundations of living were shaken. Above all the fact that men and women are physically and constitutionally different should have continued to make it plain that they were equipped to serve different purposes. But, sameness of function became the measure of equality.

The strivings of women for equal status or authority with the man have not changed. Reinterpreting sex roles was a milestone along that pathway. But in many situations, these practices are at variance with the Word of God and often with man's Divine assignment itself.

The place of the *help meet* and the principle of *one-fleshing* may have lost much of their significance for modern man, but the image of God remains enshrined in the nature of man. Therefore, basic spiritual principles continue to be applicable to all men and all women in every age and in every social setting. Resisting the restraints of one-fleshing in no way does not redefines them nor alters the nature of man.

Dr. Roderick Loney

To Be or To Become

In the beginning when God made man
That ended His creation plan
But Genesis opened the door
By which man knew God's mind for sure
God spoke and that through men of old

Prophets they were we have been told
And though their messages were meet
God's WORD was not in them complete
Prophetic word not understood
Yet God was planning for man's good

A righteous nation was to be
A people through whom all would see
That God would put forth a new plan
To reach and save the son of man
Daughters of Sarah were put in place
Through them God meant to show His Grace

For women had a part to play
At Home or Temple or on the Way
They journeyed to the Promised Land
Kept by God's power a Holy Band
Both men and women bearing burden
No turning back ahead was "Eden"

To the Promised Land they came
By pillar and cloud, in Jehovah's name
Soon every woman had cast her lot
By husband or father involved in the plot

Miriam rallied, God's people moved

The Legacy of Eve

Rahab and Ruth became part of the brood
Hannah gave up her "Only" to God
Bathsheba's Solomon made King and her lord

Yet, daughters of Sarah were quite discontent
Their heads were all bowed, their backs were all bent
Chafing beneath domineering male rule
In fits and in starts they burnished their tool

One step at a time they measured their pace
Things needed a-stirring by those in the race
Thus, little by little their voices were heard
And soon there was clamor each one had a Word

And thus it became their issue you see
That man won't make heaven except woman be
So down through the ages the woman became
A primary tool in redeeming man's name

All the world knows a virgin conceived
The Son of God to any and all who believe
He went to the Cross-redemption the plan
The woman to lead without becoming man

CHAPTER 4
Considering the Woman's Perspective

When Eve fell, God's perfect natural woman had died. In her place was a new woman who had laid aside her innocence and trusted the serpent. Her interests, desires, and aspirations were transformed. She had entered into a new relationship with her husband who had followed her lead into disobedience. The Laws that governed her status as helpmeet before the fall were no longer operational. She left Eden as a woman, who had lost her way. She would no longer be able to find spontaneous pleasure in fellowship with God and was following new paths in her relationship with Him. HIS new directives had placed her firmly under the domination of the man. *"He shall rule over thee,"* God had said *"I will greatly multiply thy sorrow and thy desire shall be to thy husband, and he shall rule over thee"* (Gen.3:16).

But in the midst of these dramatic changes, there was hope. God had opened the door to sacrifice for sin and had promised that the seed of the woman would eventually bruise the head of the serpent (*Gen.3:15*). In due course, Eve bore two sons, Cain and Abel. Cain was the firstborn but he rebelled against God. Abel his brother was the first to taste death having been murdered by his brother Cain.

After one hundred and thirty years (130), Adam and Eve had another son. His name was Seth. Enos the son of Seth introduced a new era in the revised relationship between God and man. The scriptures say, *"then began men to call upon the name of the Lord"* (Gen.4:26). Adam the grandfather of Enos was yet alive but the influence of the first created man was diminished. There is no evidence in the scriptures to indicate that at anytime Adam became a voice for God to his generation. But, God continued to raise up others like Enoch who walked with Him and Methuselah who died in the year of the Flood.

For the most part, the progeny of Adam and Eve reflected the values of fallen man. The wickedness of man became great upon the earth and God sent a flood. All life was destroyed except that which was in the ark with Noah. After the flood, man had a new beginning. *"God blessed Noah and his sons and said unto them, be fruitful and multiply and replenish the earth" (Gen.9:1).*

But before long, man's generation was corrupted again. There arose a man named Nimrod; his name meant "let us rebel." He built the tower of Babel in an attempt to reverse the command of God that men should be scattered abroad upon the face of the earth. At that time, the peoples of the earth were of one race and one language. But the judgment of God created confusion in language. All men could no longer communicate freely with each other. Social groupings developed among persons of similar speech. Eventually, they migrated to different parts of the earth. The foundations of nationhood were established.

Very little is heard about the roles of woman during this period of man's development but events in the days of Noah provide a frame-of-reference for the relationships between men and women. Polygamy was present everywhere. Earlier on, a man named Lamech had boasted of being the husband of two wives *(Gen.4:19)*. But of course, in the days of Noah sexual indiscretion ran wild. The Bible says, *"The sons of God saw the daughters of men that they were fair and they took them wives of all which they chose" (Gen.6:2)*. It is also evident that men were in the ascendancy everywhere. They were harshly dominant and women were oppressed. For the most part, the daughters of Eve were granted few prerogatives under the law and within the home had little authority.

In due course, God raised up a new witness to establish His Divine authority upon the earth. The name of the man was "Abram," out of Ur-of-the-Chaldees. To him God made the promise, *"I will make of thee a great nation and I will bless thee and make thy name great and thou shalt be a blessing" (Gen.12:2)*. But, Sarah the wife of Abram, unique among the women of that day, was barren. Yet, God had promised Abram that, *"in thee and in thy seed will all the families of the earth be blessed"* (*Gen. 22:18, Gal.3:16*).

Abram's wife Sarai was the first woman of significance mentioned in the scriptures since Eve. But she had no children (*Gen.11:30*). Because of her unique circumstances, steps were taken to have her handmaid Hagar bear children on her behalf. This course of action was congruent with the laws of the marriage in Ur. God's Guidelines for living were different. But, Sarai's plan was moved forward.

As matters moved along, a conflict arose between Sarai and Hagar when the woman recognized that she had conceived (*Gen.16:4*). Eventually, Hagar had to be sent away. In due course, God eventually opened Sarai's womb at the age of ninety. She bore a son to Abram. It was that son (Isaac) who became the heir to the promises of God (*Gen.21:3-5*). Step by step, the woman was establishing a place of increasing influence even outside of the home.

The roles of the women continued to change in ways that altered their functions as assigned by God. Events that occurred in the household of Lot highlighted some of these changes. Lot the nephew of Abram had accompanied him on his journey to Canaan the land that God had promised. As both Abram and Lot prospered, it became increasingly difficult for them to continue living together.

Lot departed from his uncle Abram and soon was settled in the cities of Sodom and Gomorrah. Some say that even Lot's choice of Sodom may have been influenced by his wife. But the men of Sodom were in violation of all moral and spiritual restraints. In fact, they stormed the house of Lot in order to assault sexually the male visitors (*Gen.19:5-9*). They were giving themselves *"up unto vile affections,"* changing *"the natural use into that which is against nature"* (*Roms.1:26, 27*).

In the meantime, Lot's wife seemed to be holding fast to her own views. She did not share the faith of her husband and even turned away from following him to her own peril at the judgment of Sodom. The daughters of Lot also seemed to be guided by their own laws of living. They caused their father to be drunk and laid with him each on a separate occasion. They reasoned that he was the only man within their range because they were dwelling in the mountain (*Gen.19:30*).

Men and women continued to marry but the laws of sexual bonding became more flexible. A female perspective was emerging that was far-removed from God's standard of virtue. Even within the bonds of marriage, the woman's status of helpmeet was being amended.

Rebekah the wife of Isaac though dutiful to her husband yet insisted on having things her way with her favorite son Jacob. In the beginning of their relationship, she exhibited all of the qualities of a wife who was respectful to her husband and honored his wishes. However, in the waning years of his life she did not hesitate to take steps to violate those wishes even to the point of deceiving him so that her son Jacob would receive the blessing instead of Esau.

On a similar theme, an event is described in the life of Joseph, which highlighted even further the ease with which both women and men moved to violate the laws of marriage and intimacy. The Bible introduces the reader to someone referred to as Potiphar's wife (*Gen.39:12-20*). She was not reluctant to take aggressive steps to force Joseph into an adulterous relationship with her. When he resisted her advances, she lodged false accusations against him, convincing her husband of the need to defend her honor.

All of the issues above reflect the will of fallen man striving against the authority of God. Sexual promiscuity and the widespread practice of polygamy became the rule, no longer the exception. Even Judah the son of Leah through whom God had promised the "blessing" fell victim to the blandishments of his daughter-in-law Tamar. She had played the harlot seducing him in order to express her dissatisfaction with the manner in which he had unfairly treated her (*Gen.38:11ff*).

A female perspective was emerging which reflected the state of moral rebellion that was impacting the world. The attitude of men and women toward each other was changing. The laws of one fleshing were replaced by the laws of convenience and self-will. A changing female orientation was being formulated. Women were also beginning to go to great lengths to enhance their sensuous appeal. They began to take initiatives that were not under the man's control.

Initiatives without Divine Directives

After Eve arrived on the scene, it seems that all of the initiatives on record in Eden were taken by her. Both Adam and Eve had understood that the tree of the knowledge of good and evil was off limits. While they sojourned in the garden, certain laws were in place. In answering the question asked by the serpent, Eve had made it clear that God had forbidden them to eat of the tree in the midst of the garden (*Gen.3:3*). They both seemed to be content with the limitations established by God until the serpent came along.

Eve was listening to the voice of the serpent. Therefore, she took steps to be flexible with God's Word and accept a viewpoint that was contrary to God's will. It is not surprising to find that this same tendency became active in the lives of other women after her.

The serpent had opened up new avenues of thought for Eve. She was stimulated by his ideas. They were the basis on which she evaluated the terms and conditions of her own living. Thus, subsequently, the Word of God and the word of the serpent were the only principles, which guided the behavior of Adam and Eve outside of Eden.

The serpent had given them access to pathways of life with which they were not yet ready to cope. Henceforth they would lean in the direction of a "satanic" bias in all of their deliberations. They would tend to take initiatives that satisfied the desires of the flesh.

During their period in the garden, Adam and Eve were guided by the Word of God. All of their directives came from Him. It was quite clear to them what God had expected of them. But after the fall it was not so. The choices they made provided the foundation for other choices. New directives were be formed by the initiatives which they had taken. If their initiatives were not stimulated by the Word of God, they would be misleading. The longer men turned away from God; the more difficult it became to turn towards Him. As the woman had moved step by step from the authority of God's Word to the authority of the serpent's word, a pattern was set in motion.

The temptation and fall brought all men to the place of disobedience. But it also limited the boundaries for man's initiatives. Without specific directives from God, all of man's behavior would now be fashioned by feelings and thoughts that were alien to the purposes of God. Mankind was morally and spiritually adrift. The female perspective that was emerging reflected the desires of the flesh that were not congruent with the Will and Purpose of God.

Fallen man had entered the state of spiritual death. Physical death was progressive. Thus, Adam and Eve continued in the body for many years after they had sinned. Their lives on earth ran a full course after the fall. But ultimately, the death of the body was inevitable.

But God had provided an alternative to provide Divine access for fallen man. It was the exercise of personal faith. By Faith, a man accepted as true whatever God said. Faith accepts the unquestioned authority of God on all matters. The Bible affirms that, *"without faith it is impossible to please him: for he that cometh to God must believe that he is, and that he is a rewarder of them that diligently seek him"* (*Heb.11:6*). Reason requires that what is said needs to be understood in human terms before one accepts it as true. It assumes that the authority of the person is a better measure of validity. Faith and man's reasoning cannot be bedfellows. After the fall, men entered a period of uncertainty and doubt faith in the promises of God was limited.

Down through the ages man has tended to be guided in his judgment by what seems right to him (*Deut.12:8; Judg.17:6; 21:25*). But, the Bible warns, "*there is a way that seemeth right unto a man; but the end thereof are the ways of death*" (*Prov.16:25*).

A new era had dawned in the relationships between men and women and men and God. The new guidelines for living were defined by God. It was necessary for Him to put in place a new plan of redemption. Without God's plan, all men would now be hopelessly and helplessly lost. Redemption was incorporated into God's Promise concerning the woman's seed. For God had said to the serpent, "*I will put enmity between thee and the woman, and between thy seed and her seed; it shall bruise thy head, and thou shalt bruise his heel*" (*Gen.3:15*).

In the meantime, a female perspective of living continued to be formulated. It was based largely upon what seemed to be in the best interests of the woman. The process of temptation did not simply lead to the fall and end there. It opened up to Adam and Eve alternate pathways to truth, as they perceived it. It also set aside the laws of God that would have equipped them for victory over the impulses that were based in the flesh. But although the woman was bonded with the man, what she willed to do began to take precedence over everything else.

Bonded but not Bound

Eve was bonded to Adam, joined with him in a mutual relationship. God made of them both one flesh (*Gen.2:24*). God had made the woman for the man, specially tailored to meet his needs. She became his wife assigned by God to be his helpmeet. Their union was intended to be the model of a unique bonding, which superseded all other relationships.

In the beginning and even in the present age God did not consummate a bond between members of the same sex. There was also no allowance for multiple partnerships in the Divine bond. In a comment later on, the Lord Jesus Himself had affirmed, *"that he which made them at the beginning made them [a] male and [a] female"* (*Matt.19:4*).

God's plan for replenishing the earth was within the bond of Divine one-fleshing. It went into effect after the fall. It might also be assumed that Adam named his wife Eve after the fall since that name identified her as *"the mother of all living"* (*Gen.3:20*). The process of one fleshing for them was incorporated into the creation of the woman. The Bible says later on that the woman was taken out of the flesh of the man. Thus, he had said of her, *"this is now bone of my bones, and flesh of my flesh"* (*Gen.2:23*). So it was that the foundations for replenishing the earth included at least two elements, the bonding in the flesh and two brought together by God.

Sexual bonding that is approved of God presupposes that a spiritual bond or commitment is already in place. Because God's Word reminds us that if a man is sexually bonded with a harlot he is one-fleshed with her (*1 Cor.6:16*). But, the physical act alone is regarded as sin. Therefore, the Bible reminds all men that, *"marriage is honorable in all and the bed undefiled but whoremongers and adulterers God will judge"* (*Heb.13:4*). Anyone could be bonded in the flesh but not bound by God.

The case of Joseph and Mary the earthly parents of Jesus Christ highlights the significance of the marriage bond. The Bible refers to Joseph as the "husband" of Mary simply based upon the spiritual bond of betrothal even though the marriage itself had not yet taken place. She was called his "espoused wife." Therefore, for all practical purposes the birth of Jesus occurred within the boundaries of a marriage bond. However, Mary and Joseph had not yet come together as man and wife when Mary conceived of the Holy Spirit (*Matt.1:20, Lk.1:35*).

Mary's conception was unique in that she was bonded for marriage but yet not legally married. Thus, her child born of the Holy Spirit was neither a child of fornication nor of adultery. But, yet He was the son of man.

The bond of marriage provides a stable framework for the nurture of children and the establishment of the family. It is not intended to deny to either of the parties the right of free will. It simply establishes the boundaries for the exercise of that will. Marriage represents bonds but not bondage. God's command to replenish the earth made provision for healthy growth to maturity as well. In all of nature, this right is guaranteed to the young. Without parental nurture, the majority of all living things would perish. Adam and Eve were ideally placed to establish a nurturing environment in Eden. However, outside of the boundaries of the garden of God they were subject to the hardships of life that continue to be the lot of fallen man.

As it is in all of God's creation life is maintained by laws and guidelines. So too is the life of man. The terms and conditions for procreation among men made in God's image are clearly defined. The bond of marriage is a Divine marker. It sends a signal that God's plan is recognized and obeyed. Polygamy or fornication establishes a movement away from the Divine plan of God.

The Bible makes reference to the "undefiled" bed of those who marry (*Heb.13:4*). The word that is translated "bed" is _koitay_. It is also used on occasion to refer to sexual intercourse and/or even to the male sperm. If this meaning is applied to the text, it seems to be saying that any conception that results from sexual intercourse outside of wedlock would result in "*defiled seed.*" However the meaning may be applied or interpreted, one thing is clear, God does not approve of sexual activity between persons who are unmarried. Of course, this eliminates any consideration of sexual activity of any kind that might occur between persons of the same sex.

The scripture specifically condemns same-sex cohabitation. In today's social climate, accommodation is often made to integrate the *gay lifestyle* as an acceptable sexual bond. Such contacts are an affront to the laws by which men and women pro-create. This aberrant form of conduct has even become a part of the accepted curriculum of some public schools. However, it may be modified, defined, or presented; the position of the scriptures is clear and cannot be ignored. The Bible groups this behavior with the vile affections among men and women. The scriptures say that *"even their women did change the natural use into that which is against nature: and likewise also the men, leaving the natural use of the woman burned in their lust one toward another"* (Roms.1:26, 27).

As the scriptures describe it, the act of sex is sacred. It is the means of procreation, man acting on God's behalf to produce life. It involves a bonding in the flesh between a male and a female with the potential of generating new life. The process is the means of bringing faith new life made in the image of God. The bonds of marriage set limits to preserve the integrity of those who are bonded.

The initiatives taken by Eve had usurped Adam's authority. It led man into bondage to sin. This act distorted the marriage principle and violated the bonds of marriage. Relationships between men and women continued to be violated after Eden.

Increasingly both men and women continue to dishonor the marriage bond in many ways. The understanding of the woman's role as helpmeet continues to be altered as men and women seek their own will. In many societies, man-made laws have had to be put in place in order to maintain the social order. But, the days of Noah reflected a milestone in the changed relationship between men and women. These same conditions continue even in our times.

During the lifetime of Adam and Eve, radical change became the rule rather than the exception. Men and women continued to exhibit sexual freedoms, which violated all of the boundaries established by God.

Nothing seemed adequate to stop the drift of men away from the Laws of God.

The fall of man was like a stone cast into a pool. It made a direct impact at the point of entry into the water, but its effects did not end at the point of impact. Rather it created ripples that keep on moving outwards upon the surface of the water. The fall created shock waves that affected the lives of all men. It continues to extend outward dismantling the moral and spiritual underpinnings of men.

The advents of the computer, the cellphone, and developments in the field of science have led to an explosion of knowledge. The population explosion and advances in communication have hastened the breakdown of moral standards everywhere. Man's perceptions of an Eternal God and life beyond the material world are changing also. Even the message of the church is being modified and the fear of God dissipated. In this context of change man's view of marriage and its significance continue to shift.

The clamor for change continues to grow louder everyday. But, common-law relationships have become socially acceptable in many formerly tradition-bound situations. Same-sex marriages are increasing in popularity and the entire marriage concept has taken on a different meaning. The marriage bond as God defined it has become flexible, loose, and hardly recognized as the process by which a man and a woman become of one flesh. The stumblings of Eve in Eden have brought about aberrations in the world around us.

Consistent with these times it appears that the public press continues to contribute to the amoral nature of life on the planet. Divorce, remarriage, and loose sexual arrangements have gained acceptance and there is a sense in which "everything goes." Even the young are growing up in an environment where values are in a state of disarray and very few forms of conduct are considered to be sacred. There now exist, little accommodation for the moral clothing of chastity and virtue with which all sexual activity should be covered. This is the age of the so-called "liberated woman." Every type of sexual configuration or deviation seems to be tolerated even within the church.

These are the times when the years of childhood innocence are often but a precious few. Babies are having babies in large numbers. Pregnancies out-of-wedlock are fashionable and preferred by many. Shacking-up, trial marriages, and informal sexual accommodation are flaunted even with a touch of pride. In these times it would seem that marriage as the Bible defines it, and the role of the woman as God intended it, have become for all practical purposes, anachronisms.

The idea that through marriage the woman is bonded with the man in an inseparable life-long union is hardly tolerated in these days. Even in many religious circles, the sanctity of marriage is being violated by those who should be the patrons of morality. Yet, God's plan continues to be that the model of Adam and Eve remains in force, one woman for one man, one-fleshed in spirit and in body (*Roms.7:1-3*), bonded but not bound. These conditions contribute significantly to the firming up of a female perspective that redefines sexual liberty.

Decision-Making Initiatives

When the perfect natural man and the perfect natural woman lived in a perfect Eden *"How could anything go wrong?"* But, everything did. Sometimes a question is raised with respect to the impaired judgment of Adam and Eve that led to the fall. On the face of it, the question may be asked over and over again, "why would anyone choose darkness over light, evil over good, and sin over righteousness, death rather than life?" It is obvious that Adam and Eve were highly intelligent beings. It is also obvious that they enjoyed fellowship with God. But they had no knowledge of good and evil. They were incapable of making choices based upon their sense of what was right or what was wrong. Their only foundation for choice was what God had said.

Although the details of daily life in Eden were not provided in the record, yet it is apparent that the lives of Adam and Eve must have been full of rich detail in the ideal paradise. There is every reason to believe that there was free and open communication with the animal kingdom too. It was already demonstrated that Adam was conversant with the language of all of the animals that God had created and he had named. Therefore, it should not come as a surprise to find them in open and free conversation with the serpent, which was described as *"more subtle than any beast of the field"* (*Gen.3:1*).

In the meantime, Eve's activity in the temptation had impugned the authority of God. She had responded as one who was free from all external controls. She had taken steps to demonstrate respect for the word of the serpent in a manner that cast doubt upon the Word of God. It seems obvious that her decision was based upon her judgment of the whole matter. God's view of the situation was overlooked. It is this action which had the most significant impact upon the initiatives taken later on by the daughters of Eve.

The woman had taken a step from the consequences of which there could be no retreat. They will continue to resonate down through the ages in the legacy, which Eve left for all women. A process was started that may be described as usurping authority. Henceforth, this process would continue to repeat itself as though it was the only course of action that seemed reasonable to both men and women.

Before the Fall Adam and Eve experienced joy at the sound of the voice of God in the garden. But after the fall, the presence of God made them afraid. The voice of comfort had become a signal of judgment.

The initiatives of Eve had led her by cumulative steps to assume a role that was not assigned to her. She admitted that the reason for her disobedience was that *"the serpent beguiled me and I did eat"* (*Gen.3:13*). But having eaten there was no way in which Eve could "turn back the clock." In the case of Adam, the process of his temptation was not clearly spelled out. The scripture simply says that Eve *"gave also unto her husband with her; and he did eat"* (*Gen.3:6*).

But, the temptation itself would have been less significance if Satan was not the instigator. It is also quite unlikely that any mere creature would have had power to turn Adam and Eve away from obeying God. The fact that they had no knowledge of good and evil was just that. They were quite content and fulfilled by the life that God had fashioned for them. But once the seeds of doubt were sown, life could not be the same anymore. There would now be the desire to explore alternatives and take initiatives.

Victory over Adam had now put all of God's creation under the control of Satan. It gave him authority, which properly belonged to Adam. Also, it transformed the roles of both man and woman. Later on, Satan tried to extend his authority even further by offering to Jesus Christ the world that was his domain. He had said, *"all these things will I give thee, if thou wilt fall down and worship me"* (*Matt.4:9*). *"For this has been delivered to me and I give it to whomever I wish"* (*Lk.4:6*).

In the Book of Isaiah, Satan is called Lucifer who is one and the same as the *anointed cherub.* Of him the Bible says, *"how art thou fallen from heaven, O Lucifer, son of the morning"* (*Isa.14:12*). The name Lucifer means *"morning star."* This title would be consistent with the appearance of the *anointed cherub* whose covering reflected every precious stone (*Eze.28:13*). The name Satan may be applied here as well since it refers to the *"nachash"* or *"shining one."*

Some of the supernatural powers of the *anointed cherub* were certainly demonstrated in the garden as he took the form of a serpent and caused the man to sin. Could it be that the evil one still aspired to be *"like the most High"* (*Isa.14:14*)? If this idea is correct, then it would be understandable why Satan would seek to make God a liar. As a result of his efforts, Satan succeeded in establishing a rival kingdom, but he has failed to make God a liar and to mute the purposes of God in creation.

The decisions that led to the fall and their impact will continue to create obstacles for men and women of every generation. The man and woman who were created in God's image and for His glory had replaced obeying God's Word with self-direction. But their initial action did not take God by surprise. He had an alternative plan. The decision-making initiatives of Adam and Eve could not thwart the purposes of God in Creation but they succeeded in turning around the destiny of men and reshaping the female perspective.

The Finality of Divine Authority

All of the work of God in creation is part of a Divine Master Plan. Adam and Eve and all men are only able to view parts of it. But man's limited perceptions can in no way hinder or divert the purpose of God. Thus, the fall of man and the sequences that followed were all integrated into the plan of God without changing the Divine Purpose. It is well to remember that even the initiatives and decisions of men are themselves subject to God's authority.

As part of the Divine plan, even before God created the woman He had carefully considered the life-circumstances of the man. The Bible reviewed the reflections of God concerning the man's condition. God had said that it was neither good nor expedient for the man to be alone. Like all other creatures, man needed a *"helpmeet for him"* (*Gen.2:18*). Therefore, it was necessary to create the female in order to complete the creation of man.

Making Eve was not an afterthought with God, but its timing was significant. In addition, the design of the woman and her assignment fitted her well into the plan and purposes of God. Even the fall of man and modifications in their behavior did not in anyway lead to amendments in the plan of God but rather an enlargement of its scope.

Remember that God had caused a deep sleep to fall upon Adam (*Gen.2:21*). While he slept, God removed *"one of his ribs...and the rib which the Lord God had taken from man made he a woman"* (*Gen.2:21, 22*). The word "Adam" of course speaks of "mankind." It is true that in the Bible record the term "*he*" is used to refer to the man. But, the man's body was composed of both male and female genetic material. Thus as indicated, it is out of that body that the woman was created. To each was given the measure of authority that was consistent with his or her duties.

The man and woman were unique among the creatures that God had made. Their creation in the image of God set them apart from all other creatures. The Bible says, "*so God created man in His own image, in the image of God created He him; male and female created He them*" (*Gen.1:27*). "*The man is not* (out) *of the woman, but the woman* (out) *of the man*" (*1 Cor.11:8*). Also, at the time of her creation, the woman was brought to the man and he received her (*Gen.2:22-25*). God's intent was to make of them "one flesh" in every sense of the word. The duties and responsibilities of the woman assigned her to the status of helpmeet to the man; that was God's order. Adam and Eve were rational beings given dominion. Only one thing was withheld to allow for their growth.

The roles of the man and the woman did not mute individual responsibilities before God and man. Each one had the right to different views, different choices, different mindsets, and different convictions. Even the attitudes and impulses, which were natural for Adam and for Eve, were designed to complement each other, not compete with each other.

Without each other, neither Adam nor Eve would have been capable of fulfilling the God-assigned roles to "*be fruitful and multiply and replenish the earth*" (*Gen.1:28*). But all the trappings of authority assigned to the man and the woman became somewhat altered and even reversed when they sinned. God's hierarchy of authority (*1 Cor.11:3*) was ignored and even mutilated. The headship of the man over the woman was redefined and when it was the entire hierarchy of Divine

Authority was affected. Thus, Eve's perspectives were formulated without the mitigating influence of her head.

In order to understand the ideal human relationship one needs to avoid the theories which seek to imply that another man would have served just as well as the natural complement to the man. Such ideas also contravene the Laws of Nature. The same holds true for the idea of two Eves instead of Adam and Eve. The Bible defines all such conditions as aberrations contrary to the laws of nature and the laws of God. There is no basis in the scriptures for the view that God approves of same sex relationships or multiple sex relationships.

With respect to the roles of Adam and Eve, the steps taken by God even initially made some things quite clear. Adam was given a male identity and the scriptures say that the woman was made for the man. In addition, the male was first formed and given the authority to rule. The significance of this action was emphasized in Paul's letter to Timothy. In that letter, the Apostle had stated, *"for Adam was first formed, then Eve"* (*1 Tim.2:13*). The processes for creating the man and the woman were different. It is the man who was formed directly out of separate and independent clay. All questions of gender neutrality are aberrations in the natural world.

But quite often, many persons find it more acceptable to limit the role of *helpmeet* to *"Compatible Companionship"* or *"Convenient Accommodation."* Of course, in such situations, the male-female bond would be viewed as tenuous, arbitrary, and flexible. The essential elements for life-long bonding hardly fit into man's scheme of things because of sin. Many mental health practitioners tend to advise couples in conflict to "get along with their lives and move on." All such processes are contrary to God's basic plan.

But, the foundations for the confusion which now exists in male-female roles had their beginnings in man's premature venture into the knowledge of good and evil. The frame-of-reference needed was not yet in place. Technically, both Adam and Eve moved into the state of independent decision-making as it were at the time of "spiritual puberty." New role definitions were needed to provide a framework for living that was more compatible with their needs after the fall. Therefore, God had said to the woman *"I will greatly multiply thy sorrow and conception...and thy desire shall be to thy husband and he shall rule over thee"* (Gen.3:16). And God had said to the man *"cursed is the ground for thy sake...in the sweat of thy face shalt thou eat bread"* (Gen.3:17-19).

The fall had changed everything including man's standing with God and his perceptions of things in the natural world. Both men and women now defined themselves in terms that were contrary to their basic creation status. Eventually, the changed conditions brought into play God's plan for the redemption of man and his restoration to a right relationship with God. The role modifications that have been suggested by the events of Pentecost have in no way affected God's basic design. Gender distinctions remain intact with no modifications in the creation model for Adam or Eve.

Much of the present dilemma in local communities arises from attempts to ignore or overlook the gender distinctions that form an integral part of man's walk with God. No one has been given authority to reverse or modify the Divine authority of God. All such claims are based upon the language of social convenience in order to accommodate the mind-set of fallen man.

The church in particular as the mouthpiece for God on earth, needs to continue to recognize that God's basic guidelines for living are still in place. They require that men and women assume roles that are congruent with His Divine will. Although the perspectives of men and women have changed and are changing, God's Divine Authority continues to take precedence over all other authority. The creation model remains in force.

Reviewing Authority

There are a variety of ways in which men have exploited and debased women over the passing of time. In many of these instances, their exploitation has carried the power of oppressive legal systems. Thus, there has developed a culture of tolerance in some situations that has made it necessary for many women to take steps to ensure their own safety. As a result, conflicts have developed between the sexes, which often put them at war with each other. Even within the church, these conflicts have tended to threaten some of the laws of God and give ascendancy to those principles that seem to advance the rights of women.

But there can be no doubt that God had assigned specific duties to Adam and Eve even before the fall. Adam was responsible to keep the Garden of Eden and to dress it (*Gen.2:15*). Eve was assigned to be "*an helpmeet for him*" (*Gen.2:20*). Their duties were the measure of the scope of their authority. Beyond that, the scriptures say that they both had access to everything within the garden except the tree of the knowledge of good and evil (*Gen.2:16, 3:3*).

After the fall, God put new limits upon the man and the woman. They were now both under the sentence of death and excluded from spontaneous fellowship with Him. Even their relationship with each other would have changed. Other variables entered the picture, clouding it with elements of shame and fear. Adam and Eve had come under the control and authority of the impulses of the flesh the serpent had gained the mastery.

In their revised status, the woman was put firmly under the authority of the man. The scripture says of her relationship, "*and he shall rule over thee*" (*Gen.3:16*). Their new duties reflected the new limits that were placed upon the lives of Adam and Eve. Some elements of these new guidelines have changed over time, but their basic status has remained unchanged. They set the boundaries of God's guidelines for living.

Before the Fall Eve had the freedom to make spontaneous choices separate and apart from the desires of her husband. It was understood that these choices would be within the framework of her duties as help meet. But, her pre-fall liberty had made her more vulnerable to the assaults of Satan. Therefore, the new guidelines were meant to assist Eve in dealing with her personal limits and causing her to be more dependent upon God. The case for Adam was similar. Assigned roles could only have been fulfilled adequately if God was factored into all aspects of the daily lives of the man and the woman.

By way of example, before the fall, food was not a problem. Eden was a well-watered fertile garden. It was not necessary for the man to till the soil or sweat in order to induce production. Also, there was no assignment of "toil" and no mention of *"the sweat of thy face"* (*Gen.3:19*) in Eden. There is also no evidence that the ground had produced *"thorns and thistles"* (*Gen.3:18*). Adam and Eve did not labor for daily sustenance. But, after the fall, the terms of living were significantly altered. The lines and scope of authority had drastically changed. For all intents and purposes, the will of the serpent (Satan in disguise) was now in force upon the earth. All of life became labor.

As one reviews the scriptural record and the record of history as a whole, the role of the woman and the scope of her authority was influenced by man's violation of his status. As part of the changes in the terms and conditions of the bond between Adam and Eve, God had further decreed that the woman would be afflicted with a desire for the man "bordering upon disease."[1] But men tended to become more autocratic and mean-spirited and the woman more promiscuous with the passing of time. Among the people of God, the Law of Moses had set forth guidelines for living. Specific instances in the scriptures

---

[1] Keil, C.F. and Delitzsch, F <u>Commentary on the Old Testament in Ten Volumes</u>, Vol.1, pp.103. William E. Eerdmans Publishing Co. Grand Rapids, Michigan; 1986.

highlighted the terms and conditions of living for both men and women. The situation of the daughters of Zelophehad underscored as well the distinctions in sexual roles (*Num.27:1-11*).

All of the assigned duties of Adam and Eve were meant to serve the Will and Purposes of God. But, because of man's fallen nature, the demands and the desires of the flesh became exaggerated. Increasingly, the woman continued a quiet rebellion against male authority. The attitude that was the hallmark of Eve's disobedience continued to manifest itself in a variety of ways. The response of Rebekah, to secure the blessings of Isaac for her son Jacob or the Tamar affair, are cases in point. Each acted upon what she thought to be in her best interests even though they may have been contrary to the wishes of the man.

The scope of authority upon the earth was delegated to man by God. But, the source of man's natural authority has changed. All things have become influenced by the human perspective. When Eve turned away from God, subsequently, Adam also did. As a result, all of the natural world was turned away from God. All were now under the dominion of Satan. Ultimately, the fall of Eve caused the female perspective to influence much of the change that took place in God's relationship with His creation.

Summary

The temptation of Adam and Eve involved elements that were both natural and spiritual. They were natural being in a material world responding to impulses that were driven by a supernatural beings in a spiritual world. The forbidden tree and its fruit were part of the natural world. But they were symbols of a world that lay beyond the reach of Adam and Eve at the time of the temptation. Adam and Eve were confronted with a choice that would have an impact upon two natures struggling within them. They failed both of them. First Eve and then Adam. Their failure brought upon them the judgment of death but transformed forever the world that was created by God for man.

The impact of the fall continues to send shock waves through the world that God created even today. All men and all living things will die. But, in the meantime, the fall completely distorted the purpose for which man was created. Eve's status of helpmeet to the man has become a burden, which most women find impossible to bear. Eve's changed nature had caused her to interpret her priorities in terms of perceived needs rather than the will of God. The headship of the man became an option that violated all that she perceived as right. In its place, there arose a new urgency for "sameness" as the evidence of equality.

During the temptation, it was Satan behind the scenes who was intent upon manipulating Eve's thinking. His desire was that she would find the Word of God unacceptable. The Tempter had selected as his medium the most subtle of all animals, the serpent. Satan continued to be focused upon usurping the authority of God. For this occasion, all of the natural attributes of the serpent were enhanced by the powers of Satan. But there are critical issues in God's ultimate authority, which could not be set aside. Therefore, Jehovah God continued to maintain ultimate control.

God had chosen obedience as the armor with which Adam and Eve would have resisted all of the fiery darts of the wicked. At this time in their growth, moral judgment could not yet be a factor. It was not God's intent that man should obey Him because man perceived it as the right thing to do. Rather, God was well aware that faith in Him was the only means by which Adam and Eve would have obtained the victory over the tempter.

Faith remains the only door by which man could have access to the grace of God today. Even from the beginning, man was tuned to walk with God only by faith. Adam's earlier experiences may have taught him that lesson. But apparently, in the case of Eve there were elements of doubt. Even her misstatements about God's initial command (*Gen.3:3*) may have been a clue to Eve's thoughts on these matters.

When Eve became bonded with Adam, the world in Eden was changed. But later on Adam's loyalty to God and tendency to obey became compromised. The man had become part of a primary natural bond with the one of his kind. His human impulses were aroused. Fruits of bonding began to appear. Thus, when confronted by choice, the woman before him became his primary choice. Adam cast his lot with Eve and he too sinned. But in his sin not only did he compromise his loyalty to God but also in some respects, he abdicated his primary role. The man lost sight of his own frame-of-reference and was unable to fulfill his God-assigned role. Relations between the man and the woman became somewhat hostile and even competitive. It continues to be so in many settings.

Despite God's reaffirmation of the roles of the man and the woman the female perspective of fallen woman has changed. It is that change which continues to reverberate down through the ages. It forms the very foundation of *The Legacy of Eve*.

Two Faces of Eve

So God had come to know for sure

That Adam needed more much more

Than animals to name and tame

Or birds to play the garden game

Man had a duty to fulfill

If he should strive to do God's will

Alone he could not fill the earth

With sons and daughters or give birth

Therefore for man God had to make

Someone to give what it would take

Out of the body of the man

God planned, designed, fashioned wo-man

Her name was Eve all-tuned to please

Programmed to put the man at ease

What Adam saw just could not be

"That God would make a wife for me"

Help-meet she was and sorely needed

God had replied when Adam pleaded

But ere she reached a helping hand

The helpmeet stumbled she had a plan

Dr. Roderick Loney

Not Adam to please or God obey

She consorted with Satan she'd have it her way

Thus in the beginning, the woman sinned

She turned to her husband and he too, she pinned

The serpent was happy, dominion he had

Old Satan was gloating while Adam was sad

And thus began the tale of man

A path of Woe, Disobedience, and "bigam"

So God stepped in a Promise He made

To vanquish the power that sought to invade

Death turned to Life the slave set free

God fashioned a plan to sanctify me

As Eve was the agent to introduce sin

So, God would now use her to bring the Lord in

CHAPTER 5
Cultivating a new frame- of- reference for God's truth

Eve's rebellion in Eden had plunged the world into darkness when Adam followed her into sin. For sometime, after they left the garden Adam and Eve seemed to be in a tailspin. Cain the firstborn continued to rebel against God and, Abel whose name meant "nothingness" was murdered by Cain, his brother. For one hundred and thirty years, the descendants of Cain continued to dominate the world scene. Very little was heard of God's interaction with men until Eve bore a son named Seth. At last, Adam had a son *"after his image"* (*Gen.5:3*). Through him, the godly influence of Adam and Eve began to manifest itself on the earth. But even so, the wages of sin could not be completely suppressed. Everywhere men were finding new ways to redefine God and reinterpret His Authority. Man lived in a new frame – of – reference that did not reflect the divine imagine.

During the temptation, there was no change in the forbidden tree: its virtues and demerits remained the same. However, in the eyes of Eve everything had begun to change. She had come to the place where she questioned the truthfulness of God's Word and gave more credence to the words of the serpent. Eve was the perfect natural woman in the perfect natural environment with the perfect natural man as companion. God alone was her benefactor. Yet, she was able to turn away from Him and make a choice that seemed to be in her best interests.

The fall had caused Eve's life-center to shift from the spiritual to the carnal, from living to dying. No longer would she be able to share the Divine Perspective except by God's Grace. She saw disobedience as the right thing for Adam to do too. Thus, she initiated sin and became its first sponsor.

Adam also, when he ate of the fruit began to look at the world through the eyes of the flesh and respond to the carnal desires of the mind. They both saw each other's nakedness with different eyes. In that new vision, they experienced shame.

In the case of Adam, the appeal of the woman to whom he was bound became stronger than the impulse to obey God. He seems to have had no hesitation in eating of the fruit that the woman had given him. For Adam at that moment the desires of the flesh possessed a greater appeal than obeying God.

Sin had exacerbated the desire of the woman to have her way whatever the cost. But for the man the lust of the flesh became the strongest influence on his life. Both of these conditions were centered in the woman and became the foundations of her legacy.

The changes in Adam and Eve made it impossible for them to maintain a state of obedience to God's Word. Therefore, the rules for living had to be altered. Processes had to be put in place that were within their range. The new guidelines reflected the different roles for which the man and the woman were created, and also the natural dispositions of each of them. Under these new guidelines, the headship of the man was reemphasized.

The new roles to which God had assigned the man and the woman were fully congruent with their natures. Equal value was placed upon them in the fulfillment of God's command to "*be fruitful, and multiply, and replenish the earth and subdue it*" (*Gen.1:28*). It is understood that the basic functions of life for the man and the woman were not interchangeable. For this reason, their creation was not the same. Their social responsibilities were intended to reflect these differences. The man was first created and was the source from which the woman was made. In every respect, the woman was his receptive complement. Thus the Bible says, "*I would have you know that the head of every man is*

Christ; and the head of the woman is the man; and the head of Christ is God" (1 Cor.11:3).

It would seem that when the laws of God were violated, man's perceptions changed also. In due course, the sequence of authority introduced by the woman seemed to be the natural thing. By increments, even these guidelines which God had put in place became subject to man's review also. The life of man became an ongoing struggle between the way of God and the will of man. Sexual differences were redefined, the principle of male dominance was limited, and all aspects of Divine authority were modified. The living patterns of men created new frames – of – reference for God's truth. These systems redefine sexual differences; limited male dominance reinterpreted divine authority and misunderstood the significance of Pentecost.

Redefining Sexual Differences

Everywhere in God's creation change followed the fall. Death was man's destiny. The concept of sexual equality as defined by God was affected too. The helpmeet had stepped out of her assigned role in all respects. The man had fully cooperated. Adam later admitted to God that "the woman given" had caused him to fall (*Gen.3:12*). Her power to influence the man established a new source of authority for the woman. In due course, she discovered new systems for enhancing her personal appeal. She was aware that the man responded to her overtures in a manner that surpassed his loyalties to God.

In order to deal with the tendency in the woman to usurp authority, and the man's penchant to follow, God put in place new guidelines. These would serve them well outside of Eden. To Eve God now said, "*I will greatly multiply thy sorrow and conception; in sorrow thou shalt bring forth children and thy desire shall be to thy husband and he shall rule of thee*" (*Gen.3:16*). And to Adam God had said "*cursed is the ground for thy sake; in sorrow shalt thou eat of it all the days of thy life...in the sweat of thy face shalt thou eat bread till thou return unto the ground*" (*Gen.3:17-19*). Both the man and the woman were confronted by living conditions that they would be incapable of fulfilling without the help of God.

In addition, God moved to provide new avenues of communication. By these, man would be able to reach out to God and enter the Divine Presence. The blood of animals was shed in order to atone for the sins of Adam and Eve. Then the man and the woman were covered with the skins of the animals in order to make cloaks for their nakedness (*Gen. 3:21*). The door was opened to sacrifice as a means of atoning for sin. The principle was established that without the shedding of the blood there would be no remission of sin (*Heb. 9:22*).

But, despite all the safeguards, sin continued to hold sway even in the home of Adam and Eve. Outside of Eden, they were confused and perhaps even angry against God. Their firstborn Cain rebelled against God's Word and offered a sacrifice that was tainted. Even afterwards, Cain continued to be angry and unwilling to accept God's Divine counsel. His anger moved Cain to the other extreme: he murdered his brother Abel. Even so, he continued to demonstrate no interest in renewing fellowship with God. The wages of sin had begun to take its toll.

The progeny of Cain continued to drift farther away from God. A new world was emerging, in it men continued to demonstrate no fear for God. The life of man on earth consisted of the things in which he took delight, even though his choices were contrary to the will of God. The Bible puts it this way, *"Cain went out from the presence of the Lord and dwelt in the land of Nod"* (*Gen.4:16*). The descendants of Cain were farmers, metallurgists, musicians, but polygamists and murderers as well. Evil dwelled in the land. In due course, the Bible says that, *"the wickedness of man was great in the earth and that every imagination of the thoughts of his heart were only evil continually"* (*Gen.6:5*). Even God's amended guidelines for living were set aside. Few were seeking to honor Him.

In the meantime, the strivings of women to change the equation and free themselves from the despotic rule of ungodly men continued to be reflected in changing lifestyles both for men and women. God's will and purpose in the creation were generally set aside. The days of Noah had come and gone: and with them the judgment of God. Yet men persisted in rebellion.

All thoughts of Divine distinctions in the relationships of men and women were set aside. Even as Eve had set aside the authority of God and violated the authority of the man, so too, new initiatives reigned supreme. The roles of women were now in competition with the will of God for man. But violations of the will of God are violations of His laws. They create an imbalance even in the natural world. Living things and non-living things are driven by these laws.

Within God's Divine creative order the fall of man had introduced disruption and disharmony. Male and female behavior was now guided by principles that were different from God's order. The will of man had gained greater authority among men than the Word of God.

Some may argue that the freewill of man is within the framework of the permissive will of God. In other words, that God allowed man to exercise freedom of choice and therefore God shared the blame. But that argument will not stand up since God had made known to man the Law of life.

It would seem that the will of the man and of the woman sprang from elements that were embedded in their natures. But, for Adam as for Eve these principles worked differently. Note that, whereas Eve was influenced by the serpent Adam was influenced by the woman.

It is no coincidence that in every generation the elements of feminine sensuous appeal have turned the hearts of men towards the lust of the flesh. The Book of Proverbs advises, *"Give not thy strength unto women, nor thy ways to that which destroyeth kings"* (*Prov.31:3*).

As early as a few generations removed from Adam the natural desires of the man for the woman began to override his judgment. Simply stated the Bible says that, *"the sons of God saw the daughters of men that they were fair; and they took them wives of all which they chose"* (*Gen.6:2*). This principle became a habit and polygamy was ingrained in the social fabric. The process has continued unabated despite Divine warnings and Divine judgments.

Two significant trends initiated by Adam and Eve at the beginning continue to influence living today. The first is the thought that the rights of the individual transcend the Laws of God. The second is that equality between men and women is measured in terms of sameness of function. The influence of Eve is fully manifested in both trends. In the first instance, it was what seemed right to her that determined her behavior. With respect to the second issue, the woman usurped the authority of the man. She encouraged him to place her offer above his responsibility to God.

Eve was created an independent and separate person in her own right even though she was "out of" the man. Her duties were primarily to complement his initiatives. That was the Divine Law of God in force during their sojourn in Eden. The Word of God had established the boundaries of behavior. But, when Satan began to contradict that Word, he was removing the foundations upon which the lives of Adam and Eve rested.

Satan had deceived the woman in all respects. In the first instance, his focus was upon material concerns but God was dealing with spiritual issues. In addition, he was well aware that death would result from disobedience not harmful elements within the fruit. But, being deceived Eve disobeyed the Law of God and with Adam was condemned to Death. Therefore death became the inheritance of all men and a carnal nature their manner of life. Within that framework, sexual differences were tuned to obey the initiatives of men not the law of God.

Dr. Roderick Loney

Limiting the Principle of Male Dominance

God had first created Adam and assigned duties to him. Then God created Eve to assist the man in the fulfillment of his God-given responsibilities. Adam was the firstborn. He had the right of the inheritance, he was the "head" of the woman (*1 Cor.11:3, Eph.5:23*). She was made "of" him and "for" him (*1 Cor.11:8, 9*). But the fall of man came about because the woman had turned the natural laws upside down. In so doing, she had usurped all authority (*1 Tim.2:12*).

The records of the scriptures indicate that Eve had moved to satisfy her own desires initially when she fell. Then, subsequent to that, she gave of the fruit to her husband and he ate also. God Himself said to Adam later on, *"because thou hast hearkened to the voice of thy wife and hast eaten of the tree"* (*Gen.3:17*). Thus, it was the woman whose Desires and Words provided the initiatives for the fall. She had acted in a manner that was contrary to her Divine Assignment.

God had rebuked and brought judgment upon Adam and Eve because of their sin. But a precedent was established which had ignored and set aside the authority of the man. It became obvious that the perfect natural woman in the perfect natural environment had within her a tendency to resist the law of God when it ran counter to her desires. Therefore for the fallen woman who was not submitted to Divine control the tendency to resist the authority would be greater.

In order to discipline the man and strengthen his authority in dealing with the woman God adjusted the Law, which governed their relationship. He now said to the woman, *"and thy desire shall be to thy husband and he shall rule over thee"* (*Gen.3:16*). Yet, even so, the woman began taking steps to set limits on that rule.

One of the earliest women to be specially-mentioned in the scripture after Eve was Sarai the wife of Abram (*Gen.12:5*). An issue had arisen in the home concerning Abram's heir. But Sarai was barren. The record indicated that she took the initiative to suggest that Abram "go in unto" her maid Hagar to have her bear children on Sarai's behalf. Later on, when the matter got out of hand she insisted that Hagar be sent away, and Abram obeyed.

At an earlier date when Abram had arrived in Canaan from Ur-of–the-Chaldees there was a famine in the land. Therefore, Abram went down to Egypt. But the Pharaoh believed the word of Abram, which was a partial truth. Therefore, he took her into his harem. But God intervened. So Abraham was driven out of Egypt as a wealthy man. In all respects, Sarai was in subjection to her husband, but was not reluctant to take the initiative in matters that concerned her welfare.

The world of Adam and Eve had changed significantly. Women in all walks of life were taking initiatives that were sometimes inconsistent with their role as helpmeet. The wife of Lot Abram's nephew also seemed uniquely positioned to influence his decisions. The fact that she was prepared to separate herself from her husband in order to return to Sodom and did so speaks volumes about her independent spirit (*Gen.19:26*). The daughters of Lot too were quite assertive later on. Setting aside all regard for their father's God, or respect for their father's person, the scriptures say that they each "*made their father drink wine...and lay with her father...thus were both the daughters of Lot with child by their father*" (*Gen.19:33-36*).

The part played by women in building the foundations of God's promised nation was significant. Sarai was a dutiful wife and God continued to use her assertiveness to assist Abram in fulfilling God's will and purpose. In due course, other women come along like Shiphrah and Puah, midwives in Egypt. They had the courage to disregard the explicit orders of the King that all male children born to the seed of Abraham were to be destroyed (*Exo.1:15ff*). During this period Moses was born.

The Bible is full of other instances in which women continued to redefine the law of God with respect to male-female roles. Abigail the wife of Nabal was able to blunt the anger of David, which was directed towards her husband. Knowing that his intentions were negative, she quickly accompanied some of her servants on a mission of peace to David without her husband's knowledge. She had heard that he was in the process of rejecting David's gestures of friendship, saying, *"Shall I then take my bread, and my water, and my flesh that I have killed for my shearers, and give it unto men, whom I know not whence they be?"* (*1 Sam.25:10, 11*). Her mission was successful (*1 Sam.25:18-125*).

The Witch of Endor exercised great influence in the life of Saul towards the end. Even though her activities were unlawful, the King himself went seeking her aid during a time of extreme personal crisis. His impending battle with the Philistines was on the horizon and the king had reason to be afraid. Therefore, he said to his servants *"seek me a woman that hath a familiar spirit"* (*1 Sam.28:7*). The prophet Samuel had died and Saul needed someone to counsel and comfort him.

Bathsheba too became a woman of profound influence in the life of David. She was instrumental in presenting the case for succession on behalf of her son Solomon. With the help of Nathan the prophet, Bathsheba entered the presence of the ailing King with a plea for her son. She began by saying, *"My lord, thou swarest by the Lord thy God unto thy handmaid saying, assuredly Solomon thy son shall reign after me"* (*1 Ki.1:17*).

Thus, the attempt by Adonijah to take control of the throne was thwarted. There were also other women like Jezebel the wife of King Ahab. She was responsible for overruling her husband on many matters. She even took the initiative in persecuting the prophets and seeking the life of Elijah himself (*1 Ki.19:2*). Jezebel was by far more aggressive than her husband and had Naboth stoned to death so that King Ahab could acquire Naboth's property (*1 Ki.21:7ff*).

Athaliah, a daughter of Jezebel, took female aggression even further than her mother. She slew all the royal seed at the death of her son Ahaziah and reigned over the land of Judah for awhile (*2 Ki.11:1-3*). In due course, the exploits of other women like Esther or Deborah became well-known. The wife of Job like the wife of Lot was willing to distance herself from her husband in his times of extreme stress.

Eventually, the advent of the Lord Jesus Christ introduced even more significant changes in the lives and relationships of men and women. He was the Messiah, born of the Virgin Mary. On His account, the miracle of conception came about under circumstances that were more profound than the conception of Sarai Abram's wife. Mary had fully conceived by God's Holy Spirit (*Matt.1:18, 20*). Thus, even in this respect the coming of Jesus Christ created quite a stir in the world in which He lived.

As He began His life's mission, the role of Jesus' mother and the women around her became increasingly significant. Much of His earthly activity culminated in the Upper Room on the day of Pentecost. At that time, both the women and the men who were worshipping experienced the baptism of the Holy Spirit. Subsequently, the rise of Christianity put a new face on the place of women in a world that was primarily the domain of men.

The rights of women became an issue of paramount interest especially in the twentieth century. But even well before that the struggles of women for freedom of action and equality with men began to intensify. As early as the year 1066 the possibility of a woman having the "Right to the Crown" became a significant issue when Henry 1 attempted to leave his Crown to his only surviving child Matilda. The result was civil war. It was not until the reign of Mary Tudor that it was declared that a woman was as capable as a man of exercising rule. Several other Rights came into question in the ensuing years; among them were the Right to hold property, the Right to elected office, and the Right to professional practice.

In the United States on the other hand, the controversy took a somewhat different form. Initially, it involved the woman's right to vote (suffrage).

This matter was not clarified until 1920 with the adoption of the nineteenth amendment to the constitution of the United States. As it was in Britain, the struggle for other Rights followed in every sphere of human activity.

Over the years, there have been significant efforts worldwide to *equalize* the status of women as it is perceived. Two primary turning points occurred that have significantly influenced the status of women in modern society. The first was the coming of Pentecost and the second was the rise of the Women's Liberation Movement. These events continue to send shock waves through all civilized societies even in the Moslem world.

The influence of Pentecost on the rights of women has often been underrated. But, where its significance has been recognized there are times when it has been misunderstood. There are those who look upon it simply as the "Emancipation Day" for women. Mary Stewart Van Leeuwan thinks of it as the time when women were able to equalize the score with men. Therefore, in an article entitled, "Life after Eden," she makes reference to the idea that at Pentecost the woman was freed from the Bondage of the man. No longer would she be limited by Religious Restraints.

It is obvious that Ms. Van Leeuwan has no sense of the plan and purpose of God in the creation of men and women. It is also evident that there are other limitations in the conclusions to which she comes. Above all, it must be understood that the God of heaven did not and would not create women in a state of inequality with men.

The "Women's Liberation Movement" especially in the U.S.A. was an attempt to strike at the root of what is still perceived as social inequality between men and women. It has become so significant that it has impacted upon social expectations in most modern communities worldwide. At times even the natural functions of men and women have been compromised. Women are filling the roles of men even in some sexual relationships and men are filling the roles of women in others. There is also increased pressure to alter language in order to make it "Gender Neutral." There is talk in parts of the U.S.A about special provisions for prisoners who are described as "Transgenders."

But one of the fallacies of the new movement is to define men and women simply in physical terms. It seems that there is no room for the Will of God in the thoughts of men. The tendency is to evaluate all things in terms of the human condition as it is socially defined. No allowances are made for the Image of God in which man was created. There continues to be a complete misunderstanding of the purposes of God in creation or the power of God at work in the world.

What is at stake are the outworkings of sin in the life of fallen man. No social movement has adequately addressed this issue. All attempts at man-made equality or struggles for rights will have limited effect upon the true liberation of both men and women. Changes in the affairs of men do not alter in anyway the foundational purposes for which God has created them.

There is no Divine plan to make adjustments in the laws of God in order to accommodate the changing attitudes or perceptions of men. God has created men and women in His image. Transgender considerations are the results of sin. They are to be viewed as any other handicap with which a person might be afflicted. In fact, some of these considerations may also be the result of "choice" not natural endowments.

The principle of One-Fleshing was designed by God as the Optimum Way by which men and women would enjoy the most fulfilling relationship with each other and with Him. But, the fall of man and the changes in his nature have distorted the human perspective. They have led man to seek alternatives that were more satisfying to his perverted desires. In these times, the relationships between God and man, and women and men have been significantly redefined for man's convenience. This condition has tended to bring about alterations in sexual relationships that ultimately are not in the best interests of men anywhere.

When Eve usurped the authority of God and man, she established a precedent, which continues to dominate human thought and behavior. The reassigned roles of Adam and Eve after the fall were coping mechanisms to accentuate the difficulties of living outside of God's will and increase man's need for dependency on Him. However, the terms and conditions of their status did not change. God is Himself unchanging and so are His laws. The trend towards usurping the authority of the man in all human relationships and to create a society that is gender neutral needs to be completely reexamined in the light of the Edenic fall and the Advent of Pentecost. Yet women continue to set limits on the range of issues that seem to highlight the image of the man as the dominant partner in the one-fleshed relationship.

Reinterpreting Divine Authority

The fall changed completely the nature of man made in God's image. It opened the door by which sin entered into the world. Before long, sexual differences between men and women became muted in the effort to reinforce the principle of "sameness." In general, as men drifted farther away from God the perception of maleness continued to diminish. Thus today, a "Rockefeller Foundation poll shows that women have become dominant in our society" (*Time, Oct.26, 2009, pg.6*). Female dominance strives towards a gender consensus. What is true in the U.S.A. will soon become true in much of the Western world. But this condition reverses God's Divine intent.

It is not by accident that God made man the head. At the very foundation of God's identity is a principle that influences everything that God does. He is the unchanging God, from everlasting to everlasting. Times and seasons will change, but the scriptures speak of "*the immutability of his counsel*" (*Heb.6:17*). Thus, the laws of life that were at work in creation continue in place. From the smallest creature to the largest planetary body, all things were designed to follow an organized sequence of laws. Failure to observe these laws always leads to disastrous results.

God had put man at the head of the created world. God gave to Adam the authority to rule; Eve was his helpmeet. Each was specifically designed to fulfill the role for which he/she was created. But as God's rule of law was laid aside at the fall; sequences developed from which God was excluded. In due course, man has come to that place where he perceives that all authority is in his hands, there is no higher power. Thus, the authority of man continues on a collision course with the authority of God.

As the will of God and the Word of God fade in man's memory so too do God's guidelines for living for men and women. As God intended it, all of the authority of Eve was bound up in the authority of Adam. She was his helpmeet; he was her head. All of the rules that define life within the house of God rest upon these same principles. The church itself is a theocracy not a democracy. The principles that govern its life can neither be changed by popular vote nor by the will of man. These are centered in directives from God. Once man assumes the pre-eminence then God's Divine authority will be misunderstood and misinterpreted.

Footprints of the fall and the echo of Eve's rebellion have continued to resonate in every generation. Therefore, men have continued to reject or misrepresent the authority of God even in God's house (the Church). It seems that man has lost the sense of "Who God is" and "What He requires of us." In the section that follows there will be a brief review of God's authority in the church and of the deemphasizing of that authority in the light of man's drift away from Him.

1. _Redefining Authority in the Church_

The Word of God clearly sets forth a summary of God's intent when He created man. He said to them *"be fruitful and multiply and replenish the earth, and subdue it; and have dominion over the fish of the sea and over the fowl of the air and over every living thing that moves upon the face of the earth" (Gen.1:28).* In order to carry forward His purpose a chain of command was established between the man and the woman. As the firstborn, the man was given precedence. The woman was his helpmeet, designed to follow his lead.

The creation status of Adam and Eve in the plan of God has remained unchanged. Eve's initiatives in the garden were a usurpation of the authority of the man. The scriptures speak against them (*1 Tim.2:12*). However, even though Eve was the first to sin, it was the sin of Adam, which had an impact on the entire world. The seed of Adam is guilty of sin only because the head of the race was compromised. The full responsibility fell upon him. Because Adam failed, God appointed another to take his place. He was the Second Adam even Jesus Christ. Here also there could be no sharing of authority. HE is ADAM like the first He stands alone.

But the full consequences of the fall were modified at Pentecost. This was the time of renewal predicted by the prophet Joel (*2:28*). Because of Pentecost, man's inheritance of death may be changed to an inheritance of life through Jesus Christ the second Adam. The Bible concludes that, *"the head of every man is Christ"* even as *"the head of the woman is the man"* (*1 Cor.11:3*). Pentecost did not in anyway change God's line of authority, it reinforced it.

The church is expected to serve as a model of the power of God at work in the world. The Comforter (the Holy Spirit) has come. The scriptures remind the reader that *"by one spirit are we all baptized into one body whether we be Jews or Gentiles, whether we be bond or free"* (*1 Cor.12:13*). He lives within the believer and carries forward God's ministration through the life of that believer in the church. The apostle Peter summarized God's process of working in the world and the authority that is delegated to the members of His body the Church. The occasion was a healing at the Beautiful Gate of the Temple (*Acts 3:6, 7*).

The Bible records that on that special day when the event occurred, a crowd had gathered. Soon it became apparent that the people were amazed because they thought that Peter and John had performed this amazing miracle. But, Peter knew that he was acting upon the authority of God. Therefore, he took steps immediately to set the record straight saying to the people,

> *"Why look ye so earnestly on us, as though by our own power or holiness we had made this man to walk? The God of Abraham, and of Isaac, and of Jacob, the God of our fathers, hath glorified his Son Jesus...and His Name through faith in His Name hath made this man strong, whom ye see and know"* (Acts 3:12-16).

Peter made it clear to the multitude that God's power to heal was by the Authority of the Risen Lord Jesus Christ.

Peter's statement set in sharp focus the differences established between the authority of God and the authority of man. It is necessary that these distinctions be understood in order to limit the incidence of confusion that may arise in leadership roles in the church. There are several words in the Greek New Testament, which are translated as "authority." The Bible speaks of the Authority of God, the authority of man and the authority of ownership. But, the authority of man expresses itself in two forms, the authority of "ownership," and the authority of personal "assertiveness"

a) <u>Looking at the Authority of God</u>

Often the terms "authority" and "power" are used interchangeably in the New Testament. Peter made reference to the authority of God as the "power" at work in healing the man. He was quick to clarify any misunderstanding. When he spoke of the power of God, the Greek term "$\delta\upsilon\nu\alpha\mu\iota\varsigma$" was used. The word points to the source or foundation of power. It speaks of a resource that is integrated into the very nature of its source; it is one and the same with that source. Thus, the healing power by which this man was made whole had its origins here, in God. The risen Lord Jesus was the author of that power. Through the agency of His Holy Spirit at work in Peter, this man was healed. Peter was himself simply a conduit of the power of God.

Other words are sometimes used to refer to authority that has its source in God. Among them is the word "κραταιος." Literally, it may be translated as the "mighty hand" of God. Thus, in either case, the emphasis is upon the force of God at work to bring about change. The apostle Peter made some reference to it in one of his letters to the church (*1 Pet.5:6*). Therefore, in all of its aspects the authority of God derives from God Himself. It is unilaterally sustained within Him. Peter was drawing upon that Divine resource in the healing of this man. Peter had access because of his connection with the Risen Lord through the Holy Spirit received at Pentecost.

b)   Looking at the Authority of Man

Man's authority is distinctly separate from the authority of God. It derives from several sources. In general, it is classified under two general headings. One refers to the rights of ownership, the other to personal assertiveness.

i.   *Ownership*

The case of Ananias and Sapphira provides a clear illustration of the power of ownership. This couple had sought to deceive God's Holy Spirit and cheat God in a matter concerning property that they owned. Peter rebuked Ananias calling attention to the fact that his right of ownership placed within his hands the power to determine how the money involved was allocated. Thus, Peter had said, "*after it was sold was it not in thine own power*" (*Acts 5:4*). The word used here was "εξουσια," the power of ownership vested in Ananias and his wife. The property belonged to them. They had the right to exercise authority over it. This word simply means the authority to choose or freedom to act as an individual sees fit where his possessions are concerned. Thus, it was well within the range of the authority of Ananias to keep the proceeds of the sale or to do otherwise. It was not necessary for him to lie to the Holy Ghost in order to withhold part of the proceds of the sale.

ii. *Personal Assertiveness*

The Bible also makes reference to personal prerogatives as the right of every individual. The Word used is "*authenteo*." When a question was raised concerning the exercise of the authority of women in the church, the apostle advised, "*I suffer not the woman to teach nor to Usurp Authority over the man*" (*1 Tim. 2:12*). The "authority" in question here makes no reference to Divine Authority or to the Authority of ownership. It points to the authority that is personal, what might be considered a self-privilege. The word "αυθεντεω" is used, to refer to "one who acts on his own personal authority" to do something that he is well able to do. But, in this case, it does not come under his jurisdiction. Therefore, even though he may possess the ability to perform, the task was not assigned to him. He is not free to set aside the right of the owner and take over because he feels capable of doing a better job. In the Church, all assignments must come from God. Anyone who assigns duties in the Church must draw directions from the Word of God. That is the only basis of God's Authority in the New Testament.

In the New Testament as a whole, a distinction is made between a person's ability to perform, and that which is Divinely assigned by God. The personal authority that comes from the ability to perform cannot seek to masquerade itself as the authority of God. Such a case would be described as "usurpation."

Thus in the reference above (*1 Tim.2:12*), when the woman exercises authority over the man in the church she is acting upon a matter for which she has no Divine authority. The authority of God to perform those duties within the church has been assigned to the man. He and only he, has the right to exercise jurisdiction as in the case of ownership. God has given to him the authority of εξουσια (personal prerogative). The man is given the right to act on God's behalf within the church. Thus, no activity within the church is empowered to set aside the authority of God Himself (δυναμις), or override the authority assigned to man (εξουσια). Anyone who puts in place his own authority (αυθεντεω) is guilty of Usurpation.

With reference to the matter of the woman filling the role of a pastor, the Bible specifically says *"but I suffer not a woman to teach nor to usurp authority over the man"* (*1 Tim.2:12*). In this reference the word, "teach" is to be understood in the light of what follows. The statement may be interpreted in the following manner, "it is not permitted for the woman to teach, that is, to be exercising teaching (pastoral) authority over the man."

Ultimately, all authority in the church is under God's control, Jesus Christ is the head of the church. The sequence of authority that is exercised is clearly laid out in the scripture. It says,

> *"Be ye followers of me, even as I also am of Christ...but I will have you know that the head of every man is Christ and the head of the woman is the man and the head of Christ is God...for this cause ought the woman to have power on her head because of the angels"* (*1 Cor.11:1-10*).

Later on in the text reference is made to the fact that the woman's *"hair is given her for a covering"* (*1 Cor.11:15*), a natural covering. But, it is the responsibility of those who have the oversight in the church to seek the guidance of God in all matters, relying solely upon God's Word.

There is no suggestion in the scriptures that the creation status of men and women has been changed. The lines of authority that apply to the church are consistent with God's plans from the beginning. The woman continues to be the "help-meet" for the man (especially fitted to meet his needs). The man remains the head of the woman in God's economy. However, man in his fallen condition is under the influence of Eve's initiatives in the garden. He leans more naturally in the direction of his own personal will.

The will of man tends to override even in the church. The precedent for the behavior of fallen man has been set. *"The woman being deceived was in the transgression"* (*1 Tim.2:14*). Eve's primary response to the Word of God and her influence upon Adam continue to pose a significant danger to the exercise of God's Divine authority in the church. But God has designed the means of integrating man's authority with God's through obedience.

2. *Integrating the Authority of God and of Man*

The boundaries of man's authority have been determined by God. It is He who sets the limits that govern the behavior of men and women. Even the stages of growth in the life of a child are under God's authority. All of God's creation is under the authority of the laws of God. But the scope of man's behavior incorporates life at all levels. Natural man made in the image of God can relate to living on both the physical and the spiritual plane.

When Adam and Eve operated within the framework of God's guidelines Eden was a paradise. But when the laws of God were violated, they could no longer be at home in Eden. Their relationship with God was significantly marred. At that point, the authority of man was established. It was separate and distinctly different from the authority of God.

But then God moved quickly to reintegrate man into the framework of HIS Divine authority. The Bible records, that God went seeking after them. Then God prepared for them coats to cover their nakedness. In addition, new duties were assigned. The stage was set for man's new beginning with God in an integrated relationship.

Though fallen, man continued to have responsibility *"over every living thing that moveth upon the earth" (Gen.1:28b)*. However, the scope of his authority was limited. He had yielded his inheritance to the serpent in the garden and the earth itself was now cursed *(Gen.3:17)*. With respect to Eve, she continued to be the helpmeet for the man but she was assigned to a subordinate role. Adam now exercised *rule* over her *(Gen.3:16)*.

Eventually, in the fullness of time, the Redeemer came, the Lord Jesus Christ. A new authority had entered into man's world. Through the church, the Holy Spirit of God was put within the reach of all men who expressed faith in Christ Jesus. The authority of God and the authority of man became integrated in the church.

Yet, at times the church is described as carnal, or unloving, self-willed, and even puffed up. All these are evidence of the ongoing struggle between the Word of God and the will of man. But, in order to maintain a healthy balance of relationships in the church God has included elements of "reproof" and "correction in righteousness."

The scriptures speak of a warfare-taking place within all men as the will of the flesh seeks to gain ascendancy over the will of the Spirit. The church provides a framework in which this struggle finds expression. The apostle Paul describes it in these terms, *"our wrestling is not against flesh and blood" (Eph.6:12)*.

As a general rule, God equips everyone at birth with the capacity to be included in God's Church. The Bible says that the light of God's illuminating grace shines on everyone who is born into the world *(Jn.1:9)*. Thus, God makes it possible for man to become a dwelling place for His Holy Spirit *(1 Cor.6:19)*. All such persons would be equipped to maintain lines of communication with God. They would become a part of that body called the Church *(1 Cor.12:13)*.

But, natural man is a fully integrated part of the natural world as well. Even when he becomes part of the church, his earthly strivings seek to express themselves. Too often, the will of man as expressed in the natural world often serves as a guide for the roles and relationships of men and women in the church. Therefore, the quest for social equality influences most of the decisions that are made respecting women.

One of the issues of current concern relate to same-sex unions. It must be clear that such relationships cannot be called marriages. However, in many situations the yardstick by which truth is measured is that which seems right in the eyes of men. A similar principle is applied to the struggle for Gay Rights. In some situations, it is deemed mandatory that such teachings be included in the regular curriculum of the school. But the Bible specifically condemns Sodomite practices in any form. The role of the church is clearly defined.

God's command to procreate continues in force. That is the primary purpose of sexual function among all created things. It is God's method for multiplying and replenishing the earth and subduing it. But this process must reflect the system of one fleshing that is ordained by God. The church is responsible to maintain that standard. Anything short of that will violate God's law of procreation. At a very early date, God had issued strong condemnations against cohabiting with animals or with members of the same sex (*Lev.18:22, 23*). All attempts to rationalize such behaviors are condemned by the Word of God. Therefore, such practices cannot be integrated into acceptable church practice.

The church is called upon to take into account the principle of one fleshing, the responsibility of procreation and all of the socio-cultural influences that will have an impact upon its functions. That is the context in which the authority of God and the will and purposes of men are to find healthy expression as man responds in obedience to the principles enshrined in the Word of God.

But one of the issues of greatest concern in these times is the impact of the sexual revolution upon the message of the church. Despite all of the changes that take place in the world, steps must be taken to safeguard the sacred trust of procreation. When this is violated, the foundations of the family will be eroded and the nurture and admonition of the young will be given a low priority. Therefore, the church must strive to create a living environment in which the will and purposes of God can find free expression and God and man can continue to walk in close fellowship. To do otherwise will be substituting inequality for equality.

There was only One Directive Authority at work in the Garden of Eden, the authority of God. The authority that was given to man did not extend over areas that were forbidden by God. Only one thing was required, that man should "Obey." The duty of the church is similar. It must carry forward the Word of God and the principles imbedded in that Word. It must continue to exercise responsibility for establishing clear lines of division, which separate the will of man and the will of God. There should be no place in the church where the authority of man supersedes the authority of God.

When Eve took steps to obey the voice of the serpent she was exercising authority that was not given to her. Eve had taken the initiative to act in an area that was strictly forbidden by God. The church of Jesus Christ may be called a "Symbolic Eden," the place in which the will of man is content to live under the authority of the will of God. Anything less will subvert that Divine authority. The strong trend in modern times to give God's Word a flexibility that enables it to conform to the standards of the world must be rejected.

The Word of God is the only foundation for primary authority both within the church and outside of it. It must be recognized that the authority of the woman in the church is to be exercised within the framework of God's direct authority (dunamis) and man's assigned authority (exousia). The Bible keeps on saying that "*the head of every man is Christ; and the head of the woman is the man; and the head of Christ is God*" (*1 Cor.11:3*). As Adam was given charge of the Garden (*Gen.2:15*) so too, in the church the sphere of God's delegated authority has been assigned to the man. The woman takes her directives from him as he receives them from the Lord through His Word. This is the process to be followed in order to integrate the authority of God and man. Anything that compromises that process is a form of rebellion against God.

3. *Violating the Laws of One-Fleshing*

The principle of one fleshing grew out of the needs of the man. Adam was incapable of fulfilling his divine mission alone. Thus, God had said, "*it is not good that the man should be alone*" (*Gen.2:18*). Adam needed a helpmeet. The process used by God to fulfil the needs of the man is no indication that the woman was a Divine after-thought. Rather, God saw it necessary to bring the woman on the scene in stages. The outcome was "one- fleshing."

Initially it was necessary for the to define himself and his role and establish a relationship with God. Then God gave Adam an assignment, which would stimulate awareness of his need. He was asked to name the animals. In so doing, Adam discovered that for each beast, there was a helpmeet, but for him there was none (*Gen.2:20*). When the need was established the scriptures say that "*the Lord God caused a deep sleep to fall upon Adam, and he slept and he took one of his ribs...and the rib which the Lord God had taken from man, made he a woman*" (*Gen.2:21*). God then brought the woman unto the man. It was his duty to orient her to the ways of God.

The creation of a helpmeet for Adam was different from the process used in giving life to other creatures. It involved at least three basic issues. The first was headship, the man had the authority. The second was ownership. The woman was made from the man. The third was duty. Eve was given the assignment to complement the initiatives taken by Adam.

146

Adam understood Eve's relationship with him and called her Ishah an extension of Ish (the identity of the man). He saw in her "*bone of my bones and flesh of my flesh*" (*Gen.2:23*). The scriptures refer to the man as the head of the woman. It seems that both Adam and Eve had understood their respective roles. The foundations for one fleshing were established.

This woman with whom the man was now bonded in the flesh became joined with him in an inseparable union. She was part of his being, more closely bonded than anyone else could be. God had said, that for this cause, "*shall a man leave his father and his mother, and shall cleave unto his wife: and they shall be one flesh*" (*Gen.2:24*). The summary of this bond finds its fulfillment when the man and woman surrender their bodies to each other. That is why the scriptures say that if a man is joined to a harlot he is one-fleshed with her (*1 Cor.6:16*) even through such joining would be immoral.

The directives of God carried with it the authority to procreate and nurture the children who were born to Adam and Eve. His instructions to them had included the directive to "*be Fruitful, and Multiply and Replenish the Earth, and subdue it*" (*Gen.1:28*). But the process was not activated until the status of the man and the woman before God was clearly defined.

The assignments of the man and woman were consistent with the form of their creation. There was no inequality between Adam and Eve in the eyes of God. It needs to be emphasized that equality was reflected in the natural endowments given to each to perform the tasks assigned. But an imbalance developed when Eve stepped out of her assigned role and usurped the authority of the man (*1 Tim.2:12*). The scriptures do not indicate what motivated her to do it. Adam's action in yielding to temptation and following the lead of his wife created a further imbalance. Sin had established its authority in the hearts of the man and the woman.

The Bible makes it clear that Adam did not "know" Eve his wife as a procreating partner until after the fall and their expulsion from Eden. It is then that the scripture says that "*Adam knew Eve his wife and she conceived and bare Cain*" (*Gen.4:1*). There can be no doubt that both Adam and Eve were created with the capacity to procreate, but the opportunity was not put within their reach until the question of primary obedience was resolved. In due course, Adam and Eve made their choices when they decided to eat the fruit.

It is likely that God's command to "*be fruitful*" may not have been given until after the fall. God's directive had specifically said, "*replenish the earth*" (*Gen.1:28*), not simply "replenish Eden." God's command to "*subdue the earth*" would have been unnecessary if the earth itself was not cursed. God had said to Adam in judging him that "*cursed is the ground for thy sake...thorns also and thistles shall it bring forth to thee*" (*Gen.3:17, 18*). This judgment came as a result of Adam's sin and fall from grace. But the entire command to procreate included the directive to "*subdue the earth*" (*Gen.1:28*).

Again, the command to "replenish" was repeated to Noah after the Flood (*Gen.9:1*). It was obvious at that time that there was no one else around but Noah and his family. Thus, God called upon them to make a new beginning. Also, the command to Noah was similar in some respects to the command given to Adam. God had said to him, "*be Fruitful, and Multiply and Replenish the Earth*" (*Gen.9:1*).

In all of its aspects, the principle of one-fleshing had its roots in the process that God had initiated in Eden. At that time, God had established the standards to be observed in personal relationships between a man and a woman. The same principle was included in the charge to Noah. Even though man had changed and the earth was changed, God's directive did not. Beyond its social and emotional benefits, marriage (Divine one fleshing) represents the only form of intimate bonding between a male and a female that is approved of God. The Bible describes it as "*honourable*" (*Heb.13:4*).

All men have been empowered to create new life and have been given the means of doing it with few exceptions. Sexual contact between a male and a female is the means of new birth as God designed it. God's gift of procreation is a natural endowment. It applies whether men and women are obedient or disobedient, whether they are saints or sinners. Men and women can be one-fleshed in the body even though not one-fleshed according to God's order. Thus, man enjoys the freedom of obedience or disobedience. But, only *"marriage is honourable in all, and the bed undefiled"* *(Heb.13:4)*.

Speaking of marriage, the Bible says that *"the woman which hath an husband is bound by the law to her husband so long as he liveth; but if the husband be dead, she is loosed from the law of her husband"* *(Roms.7:2)*. Marriage integrates the lives of both parties at all levels. They become bound together in body, soul, and spirit. Describing marriage, the Bible says, *"what therefore God hath joined together, let not man put asunder"* *(Mk.10:9)*.

But man consistently violates the laws of one-fleshing and establishes his own standards. In fact, much of the social disorder in today's world may well have their roots in the violation of marriage and the breakdown of the home. Divorce and loose sexual connections have become acceptable practices. Among the most recent fads on some college campuses is the trend towards "hooking up." Traditional dating has become a relic.

In these days, even casual relationships are likely to be based upon sexual contact. Many of the commercials on television and in public places highlight sexual intimacy as a way of life. As a result, unrestrained lust labels itself as sincere love. But, so sacred is the marriage bond that it continues to hold until death without regard to loss of love or threats of physical violence. Since God Himself has ordained marriage and put in place the process of consummating it, any and all violations are contrary to God's law.

In cases of remarriage or double marriages, the primary spouse is the valid partner from God's perspective. For example, one might look at the case of Jacob who had two wives. The first woman Leah was unloved; his marriage to her was the result of trickery by his father-in-law. The second woman Rachel was the love of his life (*Gen.29:18, 21, 23 and 28*). However, at the time of Jacob's death his inheritance was passed on to Judah, a son of Leah the "unloved" but primary wife. Also, it is Leah not Rachel who was buried in the family plot (*Gen.49:31; 50:13*). It needs to be understood, that whatever may be the reasons for choice, when consummated the bond is complete even in cases of insincere vows.

Violations of the laws of one-fleshing have put moral values at risk. The benefits of life in societies that are technically advanced may hardly outweigh the cost in the deterioration of the quality of that life. The idea of the "Liberated Woman" has contributed much to the overall trend.

But, the Word of God is unchanging. God has created Woman to be the helpmeet for the man. Adam described the woman as "*bone of my bones and flesh of my flesh*" (*Gen.2:23*). The woman one-fleshed with the man provided him with the means of procreation. The Bible says of them, that initially they were both naked but unaware of it. It is not until the fall that confusion entered the picture and they looked upon their nakedness as a thing of shame. Their relationships had become blurred; it influenced their perspectives as well as that of all who followed them.

The descendants of Adam are by nature at enmity with God because of sin. Therefore, God established new guidelines for living. The woman who was intended to be the helpmeet for the man had her assignment adjusted. "*Thy desire shall be to thy husband and he shall rule over thee,*" God had said (*Gen.3:16*). In addition, the woman was also told that she would bring forth children in sorrow. There would be a mitigation of sorrow for the Godly woman. The Bible says, "*Notwithstanding she shall be saved in childbearing, if they continue in faith and charity and holiness with sobriety*" (*1 Tim.2:14, 15*).

To the man Adam, God had said, *"Cursed is the ground for thy sake in sorrow shalt thou eat of it all the days of thy life...In the sweat of thy face shalt thou eat bread till thou return unto the ground"* (Gen.4:17-19). Then God sent them forth from the garden, both of them. This was the framework for the one-fleshing of fallen man.

The changes brought about by sin will continue to erode man's ability to obey God. However, no one has been given the authority to set aside God's guidelines in order to facilitate man's convenience. The Lord Jesus Christ Himself made reference to the Father's authority in this matter when He said, *"have you not read, that he which made them at the beginning made them male and female...what therefore God hath joined together, let not man put asunder"* (Matt.19:4-6). God and God alone defines one-fleshing and determines the terms and conditions for a one-fleshed union. Every man-made alternative is a form of rebellion and violation of the Laws of God.

4. *Usurping the Authority in the Church*

Before His Ascension, the Lord Jesus had reminded His disciples to wait for the promise of the Father. Speaking of that promise, He had said *"but you shall be baptized with the Holy Ghost"* (Acts.1:4, 5). This event marked a new beginning in the relationship between God and men. The church had its start here. God's Holy Spirit was at work within men. But there are times that our Lord's comment to Peter with reference to his faith may be viewed as the foundation of the church. But it is not our faith. Rather it is the Holy Spirit who is the nucleus, the inner core of the life of the church. The body of the church is made up of its members, those who come to God by faith.

In the text referred above Peter called a "pebble" or small stone. He is part of that rock the equivalent of a mountain. The Lord had said to Peter, thou art *petrus* (little stone) and upon this *petra* (rock), the church will be established. The *petra* involved was the statement of Peter, the expression of faith when he said of the Lord *"thou art the Christ the*

Son of the living God" (*Matt.16:16ff*). Peter had recognized Jesus as the Christ, God at work among men. It is this faith, which provides the building blocks for the work started by the Holy Spirit.

The status of the church comes into question especially when issues arise which require reprimand. Strong pressures are often brought to bear in order to have the church conform to the ethical/moral standards of the society. Just as often, carnal tendencies within the church disguise themselves as the Will of God and seek to compromise God's truth. But, such processes can have no standing in the Church. The Word of God is the only source of its authority.

Each local church must take responsibility to do everything within its power to safeguard the authority granted to it by God notwithstanding the designs of men of good will. From God's perspective, all authority may be classified under three primary headings, the authority of God Himself, the authority delegated to man, and personal individual authority. It must be understood that the only active authority from which the church draws its mandate is God's. Often it may manifest itself through men but it never strays away from God's Divine Revelation. The Church as a body is founded upon the Word of God. Its authority derives from the power of God alone.

There are times when man's strivings for personal recognition often exercise greater influence in the church than the Word of God. By way of example, there is a growing clamor that advocates the rights-of-women vis-à-vis the rights-of-men within the church. Much research has concerned itself with "gender inclusive wording" of Bible statements and the attempt to establish gender neutrality on all issues. These processes have fueled the growing tendency to replace the authority of God with the authority of man. In every case where such changes occur, the Lord Himself will be excluded from the place of authority as in the church of Laodicea. He will be outside of its door (*Rev.3:20*).

Directly and indirectly, the rights of special-interest groups often strive to be heard within the church. But it is not within the framework of the church's authority to give place to the designs of men, which violate the laws of God. All organizations which sanction the ordination of persons whose lifestyles are incongruent with God's Word have disqualified themselves from being classified as a church. The term "church" only meaningfully applies to those groups which are guided by the authority of God's Word. Any corporation or group that exalts the creature rather than the Creator is at variance with the scriptures.

Within the church the term "*vox populi vox dei*" (the voice of the people is the voice of God) has no standing. The government of the church may reflect democratic principles but the church is not a Democracy. It is a Theocracy, God's sheepfold, His earthly house. The head of that house is a shepherd; the members of that body are his flock. Thus, even if pronouncements are wrapped in moral or spiritual tissue, God's Authority is established in His Word.

There is little doubt that in today's world the church is inclined to make allowances for things that may be socially and/or politically expedient. However, the early church became well known in earlier times as that body which "turned the world upside down." The function of the church within the society is to serve somewhat like a catalyst whose principles are embodied in the Will of God.

As a general rule, the Word of God is intended to transform the lives of men. The church is that organization which facilitates the process. The scripture reminds the reader that he should "*not be conformed to the world but be...transformed by the renewing of your mind*" (*Roms.12:2*). All men and women need to be aware of the alternatives for living, which God has put within our reach. It is only then that the true purpose of the gospel and mission of the church will be understood.

There can be no "gender neutrality" within the church. The creation of male and female, men and women is not a Divine accident. But the roles of men and women need to be placed in their proper perspectives. The position of the scriptures is definite and clear. God has assigned different roles for men and women in the leadership of the church. These role-definitions cannot be determined by expediency. All men are required to take note of the Divine Hierarchy of God. It establishes the framework for all functions within the church. The scriptures say,

> *"But I will have you know, that the head of every man is Christ; and the head of the woman is the man; and the head of Christ is God. Every man praying or prophesying having his head covered dishonoureth his head. But every woman that prayeth or prophesieth with her head uncovered dishonoureth her head"* (1 Cor.11:3-5).

The Bible itself raises the question concerning the usurpation of authority. It comments that, *"I suffer not a woman to teach, nor to Usurp Authority over the man" (1 Tim.2:12)*. Often this injunction is misunderstood or completely ignored altogether. Should present trends continue there is a danger that the authority of man will preempt the authority of God within the church as a whole?

Increasingly, there is a wave of unrest that is sweeping many churches as attempts are made to gratify the demands of Women's Groups. The momentum that they have gained has been influential in setting the tone for all male-female relationships. But, the guidelines within the scriptures adequately address all such relationships. Whenever these are ignored or set aside the church would have abdicated its Divine responsibility.

Because fallen man is a partaker of Negative Life, very often his principles come into conflict with God's Positive Divine Life. The church cannot surrender the authority of God to what might be expedient. The underpinnings of its mission in the world are tied to God's agenda. Roles of men and women will be properly understood only in the light of that agenda. The terms of living defined in the scripture are intended to carry forth God's plan for the redemption of man, not his conformity to a system that leads to man's condemnation.

The church at Corinth provides many examples of situations in which social and cultural issues came into conflict with the principles of God's Word. In this connection, a significant question arose concerning a head-covering for women in worship. The implications of that question continue to be a matter of controversy within the church even today. But it does seem that the Word of God itself is quite transparent on this issue.

The foundation of the discussion on "veiling," extends well beyond the demands of a culture. It strikes at the very heart of relationships between men and women in the place of worship. Reference is made to women who are unveiled in public places. Often this was a sign that they were not under the authority of a man, that is, neither the jurisdiction of a father or of a husband. Such a woman could be either a slave or a prostitute. At any rate, the idea is that such a person is likely to have been a woman of ill repute.

The apostle addressed the question of a head covering for women in the light of the Corinthian context. But he set forth four principles, which are at the foundation of God's hierarchy of authority.

Principle 1: That the man is not of the woman nor was the woman created of separate and independent clay as the man. She was of the man as her creative source (*1 Cor.11:8*).

Principle 2: That the man was not created for the woman but the woman was created for the man (*1 Tim.2:11-15*). In some respects, she glorifies God by recognizing the man as her head (the means by which to fulfill their mission).

Principle 3: That the woman ought to have "power" on her head because of the angels (*1 Cor.11:10*).

Principle 4: That God has used the head as the place where visible external distinctions in authority may be demonstrated [even as a crown upon the head of a king or the miter upon the head of a bishop] (*1 Cor.11:14*).

In the light of these considerations, the statement is made that *"every woman that prayeth or prophesieth with her head uncovered dishonoureth her head"* (*1 Cor.11:5*). The statement continues *"for if the woman be not covered let her also be shorn: but if it be a shame for a woman to be shorn or shaven, let her be covered"* (*1 Cor.11:6*). Readers are asked to *"judge in yourselves: is it comely that a woman pray unto God uncovered?"* (*1 Cor.11:13*).

The issues mentioned above relate to women in worship in all situations without regard to cultural orientation. What is emphasized is the divine hierarchy of authority that spells out the relationship of the woman to the man in the light of the relationship of Jesus Christ to the church.

All of the issues considered emphasize the subordination of the rule of man to the rule of God. The argument concerning the head covering is symbolic. It indicates that the first visible distinction between men and women often starts with the hair, on the head or on the face. One's natural covering is not a matter of choice, it is characteristic of all men and women. However, the *veil* or head covering is a mark of choice. It demonstrates that the woman is receptive of her God-assigned status under the authority of the man. Remember that in the plan of God neither the man nor the woman become unsexed during worship. They serve and worship as men and as women even though in some instances serving in distinctly different roles.

The Bible says that, *"for this cause ought the woman to have power on her head because of the angels"* (*1 Cor.11:10*). It is interesting to note that the word used here for "Power" is the Greek word *"Exousia,"* her personal right to choose. As previously indicated this word has reference to authority delegated by God, which gives one the freedom to act. It is the authority of ownership. Thus, the woman has the opportunity to choose to obey God or herself. She is called upon to make the choice of humility and demonstrate her willingness to obey the Divine injunction. As an alternative, it is unlikely that most women would desire to shave their heads as an option, considering its significance (*Isa.7:20: 1 Cor.11:6*).

Remember too that all of the activities of worship are actually witnessed by angels. The Bible keeps on alluding to the need for the woman to submit to the man's authority as part of her natural heritage and the pathway of obedience to God. In this connection, Sarah the wife of Abraham is mentioned as a model to be followed. The Bible states that, *"Sara obeyed Abraham, calling him Lord: whose daughters ye are, as long as ye do well"* (*1 Pet.3: 6*). There is the definite implication that the woman could hardly come into the fullness of God's Blessings if she continues to rebel against God's authority.

All things considered, authority in the church is clearly defined. God is the foundation and source of it all. However, it is possible for lines of authority to become blurred if God's meaning is not clearly understood. Without the continued undergirding of God's Holy Spirit, the mission of the church would fail. In order to be effective every believer is challenged to *"put on the whole armour of God"* (*Eph.6:11*). The battle is the Lord's. God's authority to rule supreme in the church must never be called in question. No one has the authority to reject his/her assigned role. Even the authority delegated to the Church cannot supersede the authority of God. But the struggle continues as the daughters of Eve in many situations hold up the banner of rebellion against the Word of God in these matters.

Misunderstanding the Significance of Pentecost

The Day of Pentecost was the starting point in the life of the Church. This was a new beginning for the followers of Jesus Christ. Their Lord with whom they fellowshipped in the flesh would continue to be present with them in the Spirit as the Comforter (*Jn.14:17, 1 Jn.1:1-3*). The Lord Jesus had said to His disciples, "*it is expedient for you that I go away: for if I go not away, the Comforter will not come unto you*" (*Jn.16:7*). Continuing on that note, He added that, "*when He is come, He will reprove the world of sin and of righteousness and of judgment...He will guide you into all truth...He shall glorify me*" (*Jn.16:8-15*).

Until the Resurrection and Ascension of the Lord Jesus Christ the Comforter could not come; the work of man's redemption was incomplete. Thus, after the Resurrection Jesus had said to His disciples "*wait for the promise of the Father...for John truly baptized with water but ye shall be baptized with the Holy Ghost not many days hence*" (*Acts 1:4, 5*). The Comforter was that Holy Ghost. He came at Pentecost (a symbolic reminder of the Passover).

When the day of promise came, the disciples both men and women were gathered in one place. It is likely that the mother of Jesus and the women who followed Him faithfully to the Cross would have been there, in the Upper Room at that time. Suddenly "*there came a sound from heaven as of a rushing mighty wind and it filled all the house where they were sitting*" (*Acts 2:2*). In addition, "*there appeared unto them cloven tongues like as of fire and it sat upon each of them and they were all filled with the Holy Ghost and began to speak with other tongues*" (*Acts 2:3,4*). This was Pentecost, the Comforter had come.

There are other times recorded in the New Testament when events like Pentecost were repeated. In each case, it reflected the need to reassure the disciples that the same Holy Spirit was within the reach of all men and not the Jews only. The scriptures describe one such situation in the home of Cornelius, a Gentile centurion. After Peter had preached the Word to his household, "*the Holy Ghost fell on all them which heard the word*" and "*they heard them speak with tongues and magnify God*" (*Acts 10:44-66*). On another occasion the scripture describes a visible happening among Samaritan believers who "*received the Holy Ghost*" after Peter had laid his hands on them (*Acts 8:17*). In each of these instances, there was need for visible evidence of the Holy Spirit at work.

There are other instances on record in which the Holy Spirit was received but there was no mention of experiences similar to those at Pentecost. The conversion of Saul (*Acts 9:1ff*), the case of the Philippian Jailor (*Acts 16:30ff*), the salvation of the Ethiopian Eunuch (*Acts 8:35ff*) all represent such instances. The Holy Spirit of God continues that same work today, setting apart men and women who become His temples (*1 Cor.6:19*). In these days, external signs are not necessary to create faith since the Word of God is now within reach of all men.

For the original disciples of Jesus Christ, the Comforter (the Holy Spirit) was the presence of the living Christ within them. He was referred to as the Spirit of Truth who *"dwelleth with you and shall be in you"* (*Jn.14:17, 18*). Pentecost also marked the turning point in the relationship between God and men. The disciples of Jesus Christ were the first ones to be filled with the Spirit (*Acts 2:4*). Since that time, the way has been open for all men to be reborn through faith in Jesus Christ (*Jn.1:12*). All reborn persons are indwelled by the Holy Spirit (*1 Cor.6:19, 20*). That is God's guarantee. The work, which was begun in them, will be completed (*2 Cor.1:22*). Thus, the Holy Spirit may be described as God's "earnest" of Redemption.

On the very day of the visitation of the Holy Spirit, the apostle Peter had preached saying to the crowd at Jerusalem that they should repent and be baptized in the name of Jesus Christ. In this way their sins would be forgiven and they too *"shall receive the gift of the Holy Spirit"* (*Acts 2:38*). Thus, it was that from Pentecost until this very day, all men have access to that same Holy Spirit by exercising faith in Jesus Christ. Pentecost marks the beginning of that special relationship between the Lord Jesus Christ and all those who believe on Him, between God and man.

But Pentecost was also the fulfillment of the promise of the Father (*Lk.24:49; Acts 1:4*), the restoration. It sent shock waves throughout all of human society. But, the way of access continues to be through Jesus Christ only. Any of the social and/or psychological benefits that derive from Pentecost are secondary to its primary purpose. God had provided man with the means of restoration to fellowship with Himself. It puts the seal of God upon the gift of eternal life for all who receive of God's Spirit (*Roms.6:23*).

The Holy Spirit received by the disciples at Pentecost is the "earnest" of man's salvation. The Bible puts it this way "*in whom also after that ye believed, ye were sealed with that Holy Spirit of promise which is the* **earnest** *of our inheritance until the redemption of the purchased possession*" (*Eph.1:13, 14*). The word that is translated "*earnest*" (arrabon) in the passage above needs further clarification. It signifies that a symbolic down payment has been made as a pledge that the rest will follow. The fact that the down payment is made is an indication of the buyer's intent to fully complete the transaction. This gift of the Holy Spirit is both a foretaste and a pledge of future blessedness.

Beyond all of the benefits of Pentecost, it is the fulfillment of the Promise of the Father. There is no indication in the scriptures that the events surrounding it were intended to alter the Word of God or change the creation status of the male and the female. Both men and women who were in the Upper Room received the gift of the Holy Spirit in equal measure. Thus, in some respects Pentecost marked a turning point in the traditional roles of women in worship. But even so, the creation status of men and women is based upon God's principle of equality. Any attempt to change that will create a condition of imbalance that may not be perceptible to us.

It is evident that before Pentecost and under the law women were excluded from participation in many aspects of temple worship. It is also unlikely that women were invited to be baptized by John the Baptist. At those times, there still existed a partition, which separated men from women in the worship of Jehovah. But, at Pentecost, all interim walls were broken down.

Even for sometime before the day of Pentecost itself there was evidence that the young Rabbi (Jesus Christ) was departing from the traditional Rabbinical approach. He was eating with publicans and involving women in His public ministry. At the very starting point of His work at the marriage feast in Cana a woman was involved. The mother of Jesus had said to the servant concerning Him, *"Whatsoever he saith unto you, do it"* (*Jn.2:5*). Subsequently, Jesus did give instructions to the servants and water was turned into wine.

The Gospels also record a series of events related to Jesus and the women who followed Him although they were not numbered among the twelve. Mary and Martha for example, were friends. He occasionally visited them. On one occasion He even made an observation to Martha about being "cumbered" (*Lk.10:40*) with many things while her sister "sat" at His feet.

There were other women also besides Mary and Martha who were among the friends and associates of the Lord. The Gospels bear record of a woman who anointed His feet (*Jn.12:3*). Many others were also involved in continuing to minister to Jesus' needs throughout. The Bible even calls attention to the women at the Crucifixion (*Matt.27:55*), and at the Resurrection (*Jn.20:16*).

It is sufficient to say that in the days of the Lord Jesus Christ new relationships between the sexes had begun to emerge. Mary the mother of Jesus and Elizabeth the mother of John had significant experiences somewhat like those of Sarah in the Old Testament (*Lk.1:26ff; Gen.18:1-15*). Both had also uttered prophetic words at their meeting (*Lk.1:39-56*). Later on, Anna is mentioned (called a prophetess). She too offered words of thanks to God for the coming of the Savior

(*Lk.2:36-38*). The Holy Spirit of God had begun even then to set the stage for the expanded ministry of women that was yet to come.

All of the events around the birth and early life of Jesus were heralding the coming of an entirely new era when all would have access to God's saving grace. But, this access did not in any way change the life-purposes of men and women nor their standings before God. At the time of the Lord's Ascension, both women and men were invited to wait for the Promise of the father (*Acts 1:4*). The command to be witnesses did not exclude these women (*Acts 1:8*). However, there is no evidence that women were involved in the proclamation of the Word and none were mentioned as deacons, evangelists, or bishops. In the prescription for bishops mention is made that such a person should be the "*husband of one wife,*" no allowance was made for the wife of one husband (*1 Tim.3:2*).

The work of the Atonement removed the barriers and limitations that previously hindered women from full participation in worship. However, it did not open the door of access to all ministries across the board. They are free to Pray, to Sing, to Teach, to Witness and to exercise Leadership functions. But, the woman is specifically charged to avoid situations, which would involve her in "usurping authority" or exercising dominion over the man (*1 Tim.2:12*).

One thing stands out at Pentecost that carries greater social significance than others. It is the sense of freedom and spiritual equality, which women would now enjoy with men. But, in it lies the inherent danger that the Apostle warns about the tendency to set aside the man's authority on issues of special concern to women. Such an attitude would reflect the very spirit of rebellion that led to the fall.

It is evident that there are inherent natural differences between men and women, which cannot be ignored. The Bible talks about the "natural use" of the woman and the "natural use" of the man. There are also differences in the roles and functions for which men and women are equipped. What is often perceived as equality may not really be equality at all. The Lord Jesus Himself needed to remind His hearers, *"He which made them at the beginning made them (a) male and (a) female"* (*Matt.19:4*). The Apostle Paul also cited pre-Fall principles as the basis for his observation concerning the woman usurping *"authority over the man"* (*1 Tim.2:12*). In that reference the Apostle had noted that *"Adam was first formed then Eve"* (*1 Tim.2:13*), and that it was the woman who was *"in the transgression"* (*1 Tim.2:14*).

The New Testament Church of Jesus Christ is called *"the house of God"* (*Heb.3:6*). It is also referred to as *"the pillar and ground of the truth"* (*1 Tim.3:15*). It is made up of both men and women on a footing of equal access to God. It should not be confused by social initiatives based upon human perceptions.

Under the terms and conditions of Pentecost, the Bible says of the believer, *"being justified by faith, we have peace with God through our Lord Jesus Christ"* (*Roms.5:1*). It enhances and deepens the implications of one-fleshing. Pentecost summarizes and reaffirms God's process of rescuing fallen man. If Eden is referred to as God's plan "A" then Pentecost ushered in God's plan "B." Therefore, to assume that Pentecost introduced an alteration in God's Divine plan for the sexes is to misunderstand Pentecost and the workings of the Holy Spirit.

Summary

The central thesis of women in the twentieth century has its roots in man's perception of "gender equality." The principle of "sameness" in assignment is often interpreted as equality. But men and women are distinctly different; they are equipped for different functions. True equality must be based upon these distinctions, both for personal fulfillment as well as fulfilling the purposes of God in the creation of the sexes. The idea that sameness in assignment or social sameness is the only acceptable pathway to equality is the result of faulted reasoning.

The new assignments given to Adam and Eve after the fall, reflects their different functions. These cannot be lightly set aside and replaced by man's order. Even the nature of the sin of Adam and the sin of Eve reflected distinct differences in their make-up both externally and internally. The aberrations in the thought processes of modern man do not render neutral God's law and God's order. On all occasions when man sets aside God's order and establishes his own the judgment of God follows.

Remember that as "*men began to multiply on the face of the earth*" in the days of Noah, all the world was turned away from God's way. Yet, God kept on intervening in the affairs of men (*Gen.6:1*). The scriptures record God as saying "*my spirit shall not always strive with men*" (*Gen.6:3*). Then the flood came. Sodom and Gomorrah saw God's judgment too as men continued to have it their way. Men would be wise in these days to check our standing before God with respect to these issues, lest we too drift away from God's Truth.

In general terms persons of non-specific gender identity provide no basis on which to violate the natural laws of God with respect to sex and reproduction. But the initiatives of Eve in Eden continue to influence the thinking of men and women in every age. From the beginning in Eden, it was evident that neither the man nor the woman would find fulfillment without each other. But equality for Adam and Eve demanded that each be constituted differently. For them sameness of roles would be inequality. It would have undermined the very foundations of their being. However, today man has redefined himself in a way that differs from God's definition. What man describes, as equality of the sexes may not really be equality at all?

Over and over again in human history, it was necessary for God to take steps that would keep fallen man from turning completely away from Him. But the residue of the sin of Eve had significantly changed the very nature of man. He became driven by an inner urge to satisfy the desires of the flesh at any cost. As part of this pattern there continued to be that inner striving in the woman to set aside or usurp the authority of the man. Sarah the wife of Abraham stands out as a unique example of "the godly woman" because of her willingness to submit herself to the authority of her husband, even calling him "lord."

The scriptures repeat the theme of Sarah's life as one that should be followed by all women "*whose daughters*" they are (*1 Pet.3:6*). Even the model of a virtuous woman is set forth as the desirable pattern by which to be guided. The scriptures continue to say, "*her price is far above rubies*" (*Prov.31:10*). Also that, "*a woman that feareth the Lord, she shall be praised*" (*Prov.31:30*).

But the influence of sin is progressive. It continues to make an impact upon the nature of man in every generation. The foundations of modern sexual distinctions are no longer rooted in the Divine plan. They tend to reflect the response to man's expediency. The relationships between men and women are deemed to be acceptable or unacceptable on that basis. The Divine authority of the man seems to be universally rejected. Even the church is falling in line. The Women of the twenty-first century continue to have an impact that does violence to God's Divine law. She continues to reject the role to which she has been assigned by God with respect to the man.

To Worship or Usurp

Fire and thunder, a rushing mighty wind
A new day had dawned new life to begin
Eyes and ears jaded by fear
Shocked into consciousness things still unclear
Reality breached, elements redefined
Each head crowned with fire it's all so Divine
And so to every witness God gave each a tongue
A language to speak the message begun
The Comforter is present of that there's no doubt
The Spirit's controlling the words of each mouth
The purpose of God to be understood
Transforming the message all for man's good
But women today would have it their way
No power, authority, they must obey
The power of God is tuned to man's need
Not servant to whims or fancies indeed
The twentieth century came with a push
The rights of all women came out of the bush
And now that the twenty-first century is here
"For full liberation" is what must be clear
No angel or man must hinder that plan
What is good for the gander is good for the gam
But somewhere and sometime it must be made clear
T'is God, who has bonded, all men must now fear
The power is God's; His will, will be done
His plans are forever, beyond days in the sun
So let us now fear the end draweth near
The trumpet will soon sound His voice will be clear

CHAPTER 6
Contending with God's new Life Plan

The fall of man and his death by sin completely changed the nature of man. Fellowship with God was replaced by fear. Where there was life, death now reigned supreme. God moved quickly to deny man access to the "tree of life." The primary legacy of Eve had touched the lives of all men made in the image of God. But God already had put in place a plan to redeem fallen man. A bridge of communication had joined together God's time and man's time, "the Sabbath day." Nevertheless, darkness was now in the ascendency on the face of the earth. All men became sinners.

The life-equation of Adam and Eve was changed by the fall. The flesh had replaced the spirit as man's life-center. Eden was no longer to be man's home. He was cast abroad to eat bread by the sweat of his brow. But during the time in Eden, man had acquired a knowledge-base that provided the foundation for living. Thus, though fallen and limited by the wages of sin, man continued to be sustained by the Grace of God. The roles of Adam and Eve were specific and clearly defined; a new life plan was in place.

Eve conceived and bore children, Adam provided bread. The family of fallen man was taking shape. But through the Sabbath reprieve, God had made provision for sustained communication by means of sacrifice. The blood of animals was shed and Adam and Eve were covered with their skins. Like their parents, Cain and Abel became responsible before God. Each of them offered sacrifice also. But the parent models reflected themselves in the lives of their sons. For Abel it was life. But for Cain death.

Before long, the flood covered the earth. It was the judgment of God upon sin. After the flood the Bible says that, *"Noah built an altar to the Lord...and offered burnt offerings on the altar"* (*Gen.8:20*).

God's initial provisions for sin were only temporary. There was in place a greater plan for man's complete redemption. God had promised that the seed of the woman would bruise the head of the serpent. God had said to the serpent "*upon thy belly shalt thou go, and dust shalt thou eat all the days of thy life: and I will put enmity between thee and the woman, and between thy seed and her seed; it shall bruise thy head, and thou shalt bruise his heel*" (*Gen.3:14, 15*).

The world of Adam and Eve was forever altered. As the standards of morality became blurred, man's distinctions between male and female became more flexible. "*The truth of God*" became changed to a lie (*Roms.1:25*). Both men and women "*exchanged the natural use*" of each other and distorted the principle of one-fleshing even further (*Roms.1:26, 27*). A deep divide was emerging between the Word of God and the will of man. The influence of God in the affairs of men became less and less while the strident voices of man kept on growing louder. Eventually, the world had arrived at the place where men were attempting to keep God out of their knowledge. Altogether, the cycle of living for fallen man on earth became one of unrighteousness, sin and judgment. These processes became imbedded in the living patterns of men. Because of their significance, it is necessary to review them in some detail.

Turning Point for Women

The world of man had its beginning when God created man in His own image. But, when that man disobeyed God and turned away from His Way his authority was passed on to another. This event marked the turning point for all the generations of men yet unborn. For Adam and Eve themselves the adjustments were immediate and harsh. Sin had turned around the lives of the man and woman from the pathway of life to the pathway of death. Their days began to be numbered.

The man and his wife had to make many adjustments in order to maintain life outside of Eden. They needed to provide for themselves food, clothing and shelter. They had to adjust to changes in their relationships. The matter of communion with God and bringing up a family may have had its trials. Therefore, it is not surprising that their two sons moved in different directions.

A New World was emerging, after the flood of Noah's day. It was a world in which Adam seems to have had little direct influence even during his own lifetime. Man's rebellion had caused God to raise up a new nation through which to fulfill His purpose. But that man also was part of the Legacy of Eve. He was of the seed of the woman. She provided the necessary life-support in the home. It seems that Eve had taken the initiatives even in naming her sons (*Gen. 4:1, 25*).

1. *New Directions*

The Bible notes that *"This is the book of the generations of Adam. In the day that God created man, in the likeness of God made He him"* (*Gen.5:1*). But the progeny of Cain were not factored in. he was an outcast.

For a period of 130 years, nothing more was heard of Adam and iniquity abounded on the face of the earth. Then the scriptures say that *"Adam knew Eve his wife again, and she bore a son and named him Seth"* (*Gen.4:25*). No mention was made of other children who were born to Adam. Yet, it is certain that daughters also were born to him. The birth of Enos the son of Seth marked a turning point in the lives of man, a mini-revival. The Bible observes that *"then men began to call on the name of the Lord"* (*Gen.4:26*).

The name of Seth is mentioned as the one who reflected the image of the former Adam. He was *"a son in his own likeness, after his image"* (*Gen.5:3*). The record clearly marks a New Beginning in the lives of

Adam and Eve. From this record, Cain and his descendants were completely excluded.

It would seem that the descendants of Cain were all fixed on a life track that turned them away from God. They were lost to Adam and lost to the world. A brief description is given of their achievements (*Gen.4:16-24*). Their path was full of violence and polygamy, uninterrupted until the flood and a new beginning with Seth.

The men whose lives were described in the genealogy of Adam were righteous. The names of Enoch and Methuselah were mentioned. Eventually, God raised up a man named Noah for even the sons of God in Adam's righteous line were drawn into the sins of the Cainites.

Adam himself died about 700 years before the time of the Universal Flood. But God had brought him to a Turning Point after 130 years. Thus, a way was made for eight souls (Noah and his family) to be saved. They provided the human nucleus for the new beginnings of the life of man upon the earth. But enmity had now developed between man and beast. Fear had entered the relationship. In due course, the world was again turned around by sin and God raised up a new deliverer. It was he who was chosen to be the herald of a new nation under God. The name of the man was Moses. Salvation would come to all men through a nation to be called "the people of God."

2. *The New Nation*

The coming of Moses marked a significant step in the development of nationhood for the descendants of Jacob. God had called Abraham. Through him, God raised up a succession of men. Isaac and Jacob were followed by Joseph. Through him, nationhood was forged and came to reality in the iron furnace of Egypt (*Deut.4:20*). Here too, the foundations were laid in the life of Moses. The time soon came for the people of God to leave Egypt and move on to God's Promised Land.

Moses was their leader. At every step, the influence and contributions of woman were significant.

A series of events made it possible for Moses to grow up in the house of Pharaoh but retain a sense of national identity. The action of midwives, of his sister and mother and even the daughter of Pharaoh all contributed to framing the life of Moses. Before long, after he was grown Moses killed an Egyptian to protect his own people. This event led to his flight from Egypt. Moses sojourned in the land of Midian (*Exo.2:15*). Here, he met the daughters of Reuel the priest of Midian and eventually married one of them.

For some forty years, Moses *"kept the flock of Jethro his father-in-law"* (*Exo.3:1*). Then it happened. God called Moses out of a burning bush. He was commissioned to return to Egypt, secure the deliverance of his people and take them on a journey to the Promised Land.

The world of Moses was vastly different from the world in which Adam lived. Men were divided into nations and languages and cultures. Many gods were now worshipped and the sense of spiritual or religious rectitude had changed. Pharaoh and the peoples of Egypt served other gods. They were indifferent and unresponsive to the God whom Moses worshipped. Therefore, for quite sometime Pharaoh resisted the call of Moses to let his people go that they may serve their God.

Through a series of miraculous events, God forced the hand of Pharaoh and Israel was released from its condition of bondage in Egypt. But the issue did not end there. Eventually, Pharaoh and his armies pursued the people of Israel and were destroyed in the miracle at the Red Sea.

In due course, after forty years of wandering in the wilderness, Israel entered the Promised Land. The nation was born. But men and woman were both forever changed by the inroads of sin. They had reached a turning point in their relationships. It was expressly demonstrated in attitudes toward sex.

Seeking Alternative Sexual Arrangements

When Adam and Eve beheld the nakedness of each other at the fall, the place of the flesh in male/female relations was changed forever. All of man's perceptions were affected. What was morally right did not resonate any longer with man's desires. In general, the satisfaction of sexual impulse became an end in itself. Polygamy and deviant sexual behavior drove men to the moral extremities that were an affront to God's principles for one-fleshing. The thoughts of men drove them in other directions for the satisfaction of lustful desires. Men moved farther and farther away from the Will of God.

God's laws for establishing the bonds of marriage were set aside and joining in one flesh was often limited to a physical act. The Apostle Paul reminds the reader that if a man is joined to a harlot he is carnally one fleshed with her (*1 Cor.6:16*). But, such one-fleshing violates God's Divine principles.

In more recent times, the practice of sodomy or "being gay" is treated as a natural human condition, which must be addressed. As a result, in many societies the world over there has been increasing social acceptance of "gay rights" and even marriage among same-sex couples. But from earliest times, the scriptures have rejected this practice of sodomy. Being a natural eunuch is an outgrowth of the wages of sin in the world. There is no easy answer to the implications of that condition except to point out that there are many other afflictions that fall into a similar category. Not the least among those are blindness and other birth defects.

Aberrant sexual behavior among men and women continues unabashed even when exposed to public criticism. Many advocates of these practices now openly flaunt their lifestyles even in the pulpits and public schools of many nations. Such practices will continue to disrupt the social order and hinder men from becoming part of the family of God.

The term "marriage" cannot be applied to any relationship between members of the same sex under any condition. Such unions cannot result in replenishing the earth anyway. Also, it needs to be restated that the laws of God cannot be adjusted to satisfy the dictates of human lust. The marriage principle has been ordained by God. He defines its terms and conditions.

The Bible continues to say that,

> *"The wrath of God is revealed from heaven against all ungodliness and unrighteousness of men who hold the truth in unrighteousness...because that, when they knew God, they glorified Him not as God, neither were thankful...professing themselves to be wise, they became fools...and worshipped and served the creature more than the Creator"* (Rom.1:18-25).

Therefore, God *"gave them up"* to Uncleanness, to vile affections, and to a Reprobate Mind (*Rom.1:24, 26, and 28*). As Vincent puts it, "they were given to a condition, and not merely to an evil desire."[2] He described it as "the diseased condition from which lust springs."

Sexual activity between consenting adults does not change the nature of that activity nor reconstitute its purpose. Even at its most permissive period the nation of Israel continued to view such relationships as contrary to the laws of God and in some cases to the laws of nature as well. The scriptures say that, *"there shall be no whore of the daughters of Israel, nor a sodomite of the sons of Israel"* (Deut.23:17).

The writer of the Corinthian letters devoted much time to addressing the question of sexual immorality in the Corinthian church. He said, *"it is reported commonly that there is fornication among you"* (1

---

[2] Vincent, Marvin R. Word Studies in the New Testament, "The Epistles of Paul," Vol. 3 pg.19.

Cor.5:1a). He went on to add that the practice was so gross as to put even the ungodly (Gentiles) to shame.

Therefore the Corinthians were admonished to "*flee fornication*" (*1 Cor.5:11*), at all costs, and to shun the company of brethren who were themselves fornicators (*1 Cor.5:11*). In order to avoid what seemed to have been a widespread practice among some Christians, the apostle urged that it would be "*better to marry*" than to be constantly inflamed with lust (*1 Cor.7:9*). The idea was reinforced by the observation that, "*to avoid fornication, let every man have his own wife, and let every woman have her own husband*" (*1 Cor.7:2*). Again, the point was underscored that marriage is the only acceptable frame-of-reference for sexual activity. But within every society, men continue to seek alternatives to the laws of God with respect to marriage.

So binding is the marriage bond, that there is even a spill-over of blessing in the event that a believer marries an unbeliever. The scriptures say "*for the unbelieving husband is sanctified by the wife, and the unbelieving wife is sanctified by the husband*" (*1 Cor.7:14*). All persons who are separated from their spouses are expressly commanded to "*remain unmarried or be reconciled*" (*1 Cor.7:10, 11*). The Bible puts it this way

> "*For the woman which hath an husband is bound by the law to her husband so long as he liveth; but if the husband be dead, she is loosed from the law of her husband. So then if, while her husband liveth, she be married to another man, she shall be called an adulteress*" (*Roms.7:2, 3*)

Although God has made provision for sanctifying the unsaved spouse (*1 Cor.7:14*), yet the Bible advises against "*unequal yoking*" (*2 Cor.6:14*). That practice involves marriage bonding between a believer and an unbeliever. The scriptures say it would be as though light and darkness were making an effort to walk together. The outcome is bound to be conflict.

The scriptures make reference to Israel as the wife of God (*Isa.54:5, Eze.16:8, Rev.19:7-9*) and the New Testament Church as the bride of Christ (*Rev.21:2, 9*). Marriage is used as a symbol of a permanent enduring relationship between God and man.

With respect to church elders, deacons, and church leaders in general something more is added to one's understanding of the marriage union. It places a higher demand upon these leaders as role models in the church. Such persons are called to be *"the husband of one wife" and "the wife of one husband"* (*Titus 1:6, 7; 1 Tim.3:2*). But the term used refers to *"one and the same woman"* (*1 Tim.3:2*). Remarriage for such persons even after the death of a spouse is called "digamy." It is unacceptable especially for Bishops and Elders.

In the case of widows, especially those for whom the church should make provision, they are expected to have been *"the wife of one man"* (*1 Tim.5:9*). The idea is that if a woman remarries for any reason at all she should be in an even better position to take care of her own needs. Younger women are urged to marry in order to avoid besmirching their testimonies (*1 Tim.5:14*).

The New Testament is especially emphatic about men's abuse of the gift of Procreation. This too is rebellion. Without regard to any of the violations of the marriage vow in the Old Testament, the Word of God rings out clearly that *"marriage is honorable in all, and the bed undefiled, but whoremongers and adulterers God will judge"* (*Heb.13:4*).

The term for "bed" (koytay) is also translated at times as "sexual intercourse." Therefore, one may say that sexual intercourse in marriage is a holy and blessed activity, but outside of marriage it is an act against God. The bed of those outside of this framework is Impure, Soiled and Debased.

Peter too joined with the writers of the other epistles to urge abstinence from *"fleshly lusts"* (*1 Pet.2:11*). In a section on "false teachers," he referred to their eyes, which he described as being *"full of adultery and that cannot cease from sin"* (*2 Pet.2:14*). In a direct reference to the married state, Peter also talked about the types of persons that wives and husbands ought to be. Special mention was made of the modes of dress, manner, and general attitude of the wife (*1 Pet.3:1-6*). In his counsel to husbands he made it abundantly clear that even the prayers of the husband could be hindered by improper relationships with his wife within a marriage (*1 Pet.3:7*).

One of the high points of the Book of Revelation is the Marriage Supper of the Lamb. The Lamb's wife is symbolically, the church (*Rev.19:7-9*). The Book of Genesis began to unfold with the Marriage of Adam and Eve. The Book of Revelation closes upon the Spiritual Marriage between Jesus Christ and His Church. Thus, the Bible begins and ends with Marriage. *"The first man Adam was a living soul; the last Adam* (the Lord Jesus) *was made a quickening spirit"* (*1 Cor.15:45*). There can be No Alternative Sexual Arrangements that are Acceptable to God outside of the marriage bond. But men and women continue to look with favor on such practices.

Setting aside the Principles Governing Marriage

The Bible presents several basic principles that lie at the foundations of marriage. God's intent was to provide the means by which men could multiply, replenish and subdue the earth. As the Bible defines marriage, it was established to provide man with the means of fulfilling his earthly mission. Essentially, it is the means of carrying forward two of man's basic responsibilities on earth, replenishing and nurture. The Lord Himself noted that in heaven there is no marrying or giving in marriage (*Matt.24:38*). But like all of the laws of God marriage is founded upon certain principles. When these are violated then the purposes for marriage cannot be fulfilled.

There is a continuing drift away from God's Word to man's perspective even within the church itself. Therefore, it is necessary to take another look at the institution of marriage as God intended it. The elements that entered into God's design have in no way been modified. To ignore them or strive to lay them aside is to continue the on-going rebellion against the Creator. In the plan of God Nature and Nurture are predominant.

Nature

It was by Divine Decree that all men are made in the image and nature of God. Marriage provides the Divine framework in which to exercise God's Gift of procreation. Thus, the children of such unions will be born into an environment that is morally compatible with the Divine Will and Purpose. Since man unlike all other creatures is a Moral being, his natural environment will include those elements that are tuned to God's Moral Nature.

It is important that everything within the environment of the child underscore his spiritual heritage and responsibility. In this way self-perceptions will emerge that identify the child with both the physical and spiritual nature of his being.

Nurture

The mother is the parent of primary consideration both in nature and in nurture. Unlike the young in the kingdom of animals, children have an extended period of development. They require many years of nurturing to reach maturity. During the time of growth, the home must be stable enough to provide the basic elements that are necessary to sustain life and develop healthy adults. Their physical, mental, spiritual and moral growth is vital to the life of the community. Where any of these elements are lacking both the child and the society will suffer. In almost every situation, the daughters of Eve exercise a stabilizing influence in the home.

The world in which we live is currently undergoing a period of lawlessness and moral irresponsibility that relate directly to the breakdown of the traditional family and the home. Because of the nature of man, nurture is vital for the child. Both nature and nurture form the foundation for the life of man on earth. These are two of the primary principles governing marriage. Yet there is a striving to set them aside or ignore them altogether.

Because God is not in all of man's thoughts, it is natural for the unregenerate to go "his way." Therefore, the heart that is fixed in unbelief has no avenue by which to hear God's voice or understand God's meaning. But there is no plan of man, which is able to sanctify sin whether it is willful, or in ignorance. There are no terms in the scriptures, which accommodate alternative sexual conduct or *convenient* alternative life-styles for any reason. Marriage is sacred and binding. Without it social systems will simply fall apart.

On the face of it some of the principles set forth in the New Testament seem to be in conflict with Old Testament. Marriage relationships then allowed for much flexibility with respect to the behavior of the husband. But the Bible is quick to observe that Moses made these adjustments because of the "hardness" of the hearts of the people. However, that which was from the beginning was still applicable and in force (*Matt.19:8*). Our Lord Jesus Christ Himself underscored its importance when He said *"what therefore God hath joined together let not man put asunder"* (*Matt.19:5*).

After Pentecost, the New Testament became more specific in its recommendations for strengthening marriages. In almost every letter to the churches, a strong admonition was given to flee loose sexual relationships (*1 Cor.6, 10, Gal.5, Eph.5, Col.3, 1 Thess.4, 2 Tim.2, Heb.12, 1 Pet.2*). It seems that more homes are broken by sexual intimacy outside of marriage than any other single factor. But one needs to be continually reminded of the axiom in the book of Hebrews, that, *"marriage is honorable in all, and the bed undefiled"* (*Heb.13:4*).

178

The entire record of scripture echoes one common theme with respect to intimate relationships between men and women. It is that men should separate themselves from activity that brings dishonor to the body and dishonors God (*1 Cor.6:15, 19*). Of course, the presumption of scripture is that marriage is impossible between same-sex couples.

The Bible is also specific in saying that *"every sin that a man doeth is without the body; but he that committeth fornication sinneth against his own body"* (*1 Cor.6:18*). The emphasis in all sexual relationships is that men fulfill the purposes of his Creator and continue God's mandate for replenishing the earth. Sexual organs are sacred. Even the ungodly bring forth children who are made in God's image. But, in general terms, man has tended to upgrade the pleasure component in sexual relationships and downplay the intent and purposes of God. Thus, there has developed a culture of sexual pleasure as an end in itself, not the means to an end.

Sex is the means designed for the reproduction of life in all living things. Man is no exception. But God has empowered man to replenish the earth by the process of pro-creation and also to subdue it (*Gen.1:28*). The urge to reproduce is a driving force in all living things. But man made in the image of God produces life in the image of God. This is a sacred responsibility, which is violated when life-producing contacts are abused. Unfortunately, the Fall of man brought all of his human impulses under the control of sin. Therefore, what now seems to be right to the natural man will always run counter to the will and purpose of God.

There are times when even legitimate marriages are used as opportunities for sexual or social exploitation. But, one fleshing in marriage transforms a casual friendship between two persons into the nucleus of blood relationships and the closest earthly human ties. In the New Testament, priorities are established in marriage that take precedence over all other relationships. Marriage incorporates elements of Blending, Bonding, Blood-linking and Bending persons of different backgrounds. It creates the environment in which each child may be nurtured or equipped to fulfill God's command to Adam. When the elements that constitute marriage are brushed aside or ignored children suffer and the world itself suffers loss.

Denying the Inevitable

The marriage principle is based upon the sense that for every needy Adam there is somewhere a needy Eve. There was no place in the plan of God for alternatives "then" and there is no place for alternatives "now." The terms "bigamy" and "digamy" both emphasize and define the boundaries established by God to preserve the marriage union.

For as long as they live every Adam will be of one-flesh with his Eve. The primary model for the creation of the woman emphasizes that fact. Eve could not "unflesh" herself from the man out of whom her flesh was taken. The issue of one-fleshing with a harlot violates the image of God in man. It is a mutation of the human spirit.

Marriage by all accounts is the Divine marker for one-fleshing. It involves a process of Blending of Orientations, Bonding of those involved and establishing new blood lines. To deny that these things happen is an attempt to screen out the inevitable.

1. *Blending Talents*

Marriage brings together a male and a female often from different backgrounds and with different interests. It provides the framework for blending differences into one common purpose. In some respects, each marriage partner serves as a type of "file" with abrasive edges to grind down elements in the other that hinder communication. The marriage union provides the framework for an integration of two lives, a fusion of interests, tastes, and resources. Thus, over time adjustments take place that establish the foundations for a family and provide the building blocks for a society.

In some societies, there is the practice of dating. This process is intended to establish an information base to facilitate adjustments after vows are taken. But, too often it facilitates sexual intimacy before bonding. The practice in modern times does not serve the best interests of any couple. Rather, it tends to undermine the process of maturing love, thus causing emotions to crest prematurely. Dating contributes to a familiarity, which often places emotional fulfillment before commitment. There is no available data to document the truth of this observation. But the record of broken marriages speaks volumes.

Unless and until the will to do or to perform is ceded one to the other, internal relationships will soon fall apart and discontinue altogether. Even personal values need to be revised in the process of meeting each other's needs. Beyond all these things marriage provides scope for a spiritual integration that also influences values. These extend beyond the range of material things to build a moral-philosophical foundation for living that is necessary in the nurturing environment of children.

2. *Bonding Lives*

The marriage bond makes of two persons (a man, and a woman) one flesh, or one being. It duplicates all over again the process by which God created woman. When a man and woman commit themselves to each other as God has intended, they too become "of one flesh." This bond may take place among all persons without regard to racial or cultural differences.

Bonding establishes an invisible union that transcends observable physical differences. There is a spiritual element within a man, which seeks its complement in the woman. Incomplete bonding will inhibit that search for fulfillment.

To be one fleshed only in the body establishes a loose relationship. It violates the marriage bond and makes a mockery of the intent and purpose of one fleshing. God's order of things was intended to facilitate man's empowerment to procreate, replenish, and subdue the earth within the framework of compatible companionship.

The life of the Woman at the Well who met Jesus Christ underscores the differences between marriage and a loose sexual arrangement. She could safely say that she had no husband or was unattached yet she was one fleshed in the body with more than one man (*Jn.4:18*). She did not seem to have bonded loyalties to anyone. If children were involved, their interests were not high on her agenda. But the marriage bond requires the surrender of many of the individual freedoms, which this woman had not relinquished before she met Jesus Christ.

3. *Linking Bloods*

The Bible says that God *"hath made of one blood all nations of men for to dwell on all the face of the earth"* (*Acts 17:26*). This is a common bond that links all members of the human race. Every nation and every tribe is part of the common heritage of Adam. This is the fact that makes it possible for the Blood of Jesus Christ to effectively atone for the sin of all men.

But the birth of a child is the linking of two bloods. Yet that new birth also marks the beginning of a new blood-line, which did not exist before. Whatever may be the distinctions between the mother and the father the child establishes something unique. This process is repeated at the birth of each child. In this way marriage provides the foundation out of which all the peoples of the earth emerged from one man and one woman at the beginning.

The new life that emerges out of two persons will itself become the starting point of new generations that may be distinctly different from its forbears. This is the system that makes all men brethren, linked to a common ancestor. Language, culture, and race provide a social divide. But the bond of marriage blends two into one, linking bloods and bringing forth new lives into the family of men. In every sense of the word marriage is the framework for reinforcing the principle that God has made all men of one blood (*Acts 17:26*). Adam could not get the process going until Eve came along.

Summary

The interactions between man and woman are best managed when they are truly of one flesh. But even so, man and woman continually strive to alter God's life plan to make it compatible with their own desires. One of the primary issues that a man and woman bonded in marriage face is the challenge of bending one will to the will of another. The process of making decisions brings differences into focus. When two people are involved, a new system has to be designed for arriving at a consensus. This process tests all of the attitudes that influence the human will. Opportunities arise in marriage for the development of humility, which gives first consideration to the other. The exercises of the duties of headship or helpmeet require a measure of maturity that is sufficient to enable one to give place to the other.

In all its respects, marriage involves bending, or making concessions one for the other. It forms the nucleus of God's life plan for man. No allowance or provision is made for permanent separations that result in remarriage. A spouse becomes a life investment. The scriptures keep on repeating the principle of the permanence of marriage. When the paths of the man and his wife lead in directions that separate them, the impact is particularly devastating for the children of the household.

But, the wife must care enough and trust enough to submit to the authority of her husband. The husband must love enough and be concerned enough to be patient with his wife. Each must constantly bend to the will of the other in order to avoid the paths that lead to bitterness or recrimination   (*Eph.5:22-23; Col.3:18, 19; Titus 2:4; 1 Pet.3:1-7*).

Yet, even under optimum conditions, differences will arise between those whom God has joined together. These differences should be resolved "with all deliberate speed." Unresolved differences are likely to blossom into conflicts. The scriptural admonition advises, *"be ye angry, and sin not; let not the sun go down upon your wrath; neither give place to the devil"* (*Eph.4:26, 27*). Even simple differences of opinion may become roots of bitterness if they are not quickly healed. But the times in which we live give priority to the rights of the individual even at the expense of the marriage bond.

Therefore, in most western countries divorce is on the rise. Many couples seem unwilling to adjust to the discipline of marriage. As a general rule, the emphasis upon sex in the larger community has had a strong influence on the attitudes of men and women even within the bonds of marriage. Despite the confusion about sexual relationships and loose arrangements within the same sex, the sanctity of marriage must be underscored.

Much of marriage bonding is linked to the model that is presented in God's Word. The man and the woman who are joined in matrimony are bound by the laws of God. However, quite often, these laws are cast aside and sexual distinctions are ignored. Such considerations create imbalances in the bonding relationship. In large measure, they continue to contribute to the incidence of broken homes, child delinquency, and general deterioration of the social structure.

The accounts given of Eden and the place of Adam and Eve in God's creative plan are not fairy tales. The experiences of the man and the woman provide insights into their characters and call attention to the uniqueness of their creation. But when sin entered the picture because of the fall, their differences were exacerbated. Henceforth, their weaknesses not their strengths became the driving force in shaping their behavior. Man had entered a process of negative life.

While they were in the Garden, the commitments of Adam and Eve to each other faced no serious threats until the fall. Subsequently, they saw each other as naked and moved to conceal their nakedness one from the other. They had turned away from the path of life with God. They left the garden as a couple who had failed and were now sinners. What they passed on to their offspring reflected their condition. From that day forward there continued to be a progression of evil. By the time, men began to multiply upon the face of the earth, "*and daughters were born to them*" the heart of man had become completely alienated from God (*Gen.6:1*).

Despite all of the Laws of God under the Mosaic economy, men in every walk of life continued to wrestle with the power and pull of the flesh. Even Moses himself was at times frustrated in his attempts to "contain" and "accommodate" the sinful impulses of men and women whose hearts were turning away from Jehovah. Relevant laws were established, but these too often failed.

The birth of Israel as a nation whose God is the Lord did not shield God's people from the influence of sin. The Bible says that they literally went a-whoring after other gods. God's people themselves became carnal and confused, requiring special laws to deal with their sexual aberrations. Sodomy, harlotry, fornication, and adultery manifested themselves everywhere. Man was rejecting the guidelines for living established by God. Even the natural distinctions between men and women were often blurred. Rebellion against God the Creator was moving along at a fast pace. The primary initiatives of Eve were gaining momentum as men kept on contending with God's life plan.

The Legacy of Eve

Eve Unbound

Not long it took the world to see
That Eve had left a legacy
A path to tread, a role to play
For man and woman of each day

Though one-fleshed she, "help-meet" to be
Resisted all authority
Would turn the rules both up and down
Around them a way must be found

That Eve might do her own desire
Come death or even come Hell-fire
Her mind was bent on being free
From what she saw as not to be

Before no man would she yet bow
Despite her promise, pledge, or vow
She thought within herself that she
Would have the fruit "Pure Ecstasy"

She stretched her hand took of the tree
Ate of the fruit that should not be
And then to Adam quickly turned
Fearful, unsure, the morsel burned

"Help me" she says "turn not away
Come walk with me please let us stray"
He shuddered briefly at the thought
And then seduced no longer fought
Thus was it then the man was bought

But God has found a way to be

Dr. Roderick Loney

Man may have power over ecstasy
Transvestites are now off their game
Men and women are not the same

But yet with daughters everywhere
Too many Eves tempt man to share
Though Abraham had an Alternate
And David took Bathsheba's gate

The plan of God will man fulfill
When one-fleshed in the Divine will
God's Spirit working in the world
All broken men now to be whole

Adam's unbound completely, fully free
And Eve now has new Destiny
For sin has changed the roles of man
Living is now contrary to the Divine plan

CONCLUSION

Quite often, the term Legacy is used to refer to something substantial that is received from a predecessor. But, the life of every man is itself a Legacy for others especially his children. But each life is a summary of the footprints of predecessors bonded with my own. For Adam and Eve things were different their legacy was shaped only by the things, which they had done. There was none to precede them. Their lives marked the beginning of the history of man. The things that they have done provide a general frame – of – reference which has made its impact on the lives of all women and men. The Legacy of Eve from the beginning has modeled the lives of men and women in a way that provided a framework for living.

But Eve was created for the glory of man and Adam for the Glory of God. This distinction had its impact on the foundations of the nature on all, men and women. Even from the beginning in Eden, the woman was able to lead the man to turn away from God.

Legacies cannot be modified or changed in any way after the death of the testator. That is also true of the Legacy of Eve, the first woman. Her words and deeds have had a paramount influence on how women have defined themselves. But not only so, her strengths and her weaknesses, her successes and her failures have also influenced the way in which men have defined themselves too.

The Bible maintains that *"in the beginning God created the heaven and the earth"* (*Gen.1:1*), no "ifs" or "ands" or "buts." It affirms that this same God *"created man in his own image, in the image of God created he him; male and female created he them"* (*Gen.1:27*). There is no evidence to provide a foundation for any alternative claims concerning how it all began. Adam and Eve were the male and female whom God had created. The man and the woman each had a different role to play in the plan of God. But, the fall of Eve opened the door to sin, to man-made alternatives and to the heritage of Death.

189

By all accounts, it would seem that the Garden of Eden was the perfect natural environment in which to nurture a relationship between man and God. Here God had placed the perfect natural man and the perfect natural woman bonded together in the perfect union, of one flesh. Apart from the responsibilities assigned to each, the man and the woman were warned against eating of the tree of the knowledge of good and evil. Their claims to life depended upon their obedience to God's command.

Before Eve came along there is reason to believe Adam's fellowship with God was unbroken. The coming of Eve provided an outlet by which the man was able to communicate with one of his own kind. But, she also provided companionship and supplementary fellowship. Might there have been an element that developed in the man's relationship with the woman from which God was excluded?

The account in the Genesis record reveals Adam's high level of excitement when he saw Eve. He seemed literally to be "falling all over her." The male had found his female counterpart. She was that unit that matched to perfection all of the man's earthly needs. Eve was the necessary complement to enable the man to fulfill God's command to be fruitful and multiply and replenish the earth. She was *out of* the man and *for* the man.

There was something in the nature of the woman that created sensuous appeal for Adam. At the invitation to eat with her, the man seems to have yielded himself without question or second thoughts. Later on, when God enquired Adam had said that *"the woman whom thou gavest to be with me, she gave me"* (Gen.3:12). What is this power that the woman seems to have wielded over the man? And so it is that the record of man's history includes many instances in which men have been seduced by women over and over again.

Before Adam and Eve could begin to obey God's command "to multiply," they were called upon to obey God's Law of life. Each was responsible for making his own decision independent of the other. God's place in each life needed to be clearly established. No specific time limit was placed upon obedience. The Bible did not spell out the time-lapse between obedience and disobedience. But, God had said that, if they had eaten of the forbidden tree they would certainly die.

The tree of the knowledge of good and evil was God's testing ground for man. It is also likely that the tree possessed properties, which made it more attractive to man than the tree of life. But, its exotic appeal only became apparent when Eve was stimulated to consider its virtues. As she looked again at that which was forbidden, she was overwhelmed. Her instincts were aroused and she partook of it. Her action opened the door to an alternative way. Her husband Adam followed her. He was faced with the prospect of returning to a life without the woman. He chose the woman.

It is understood that what God had said to Adam concerning the "Forbidden Tree," Eve surely knew. She was well aware of her responsibility in this matter. She even spoke confidently to the serpent about what God had said even though her wording was a bit different. Could it be that even then Eve was unclear about the certainty of death. Did she come to believe that it was possible but not necessarily inevitable?

Instructions in righteousness began for Adam and Eve from the day that God created them. He knew that the enemy was lurking in the garden. He had prepared them for the encounter by requiring their obedience. Everything seemed to be working quite well in paradise for awhile. But then the serpent became aggressive. Satan had entered into him and enhanced his knowledge and natural abilities. The stage was set.

For the serpent, Eve was an easier target. She knew nothing about his character as Adam did. At first, he came to her under the guise of seeking information. His opening question to Eve was, *"Yea, hath God said ye shall not eat of every tree of the garden?"* (*Gen.3:1*). She fell into the trap and responded as he had expected. But, reacting to her reply, the serpent demonstrated his prior knowledge of what God really did say. He said to Eve, "*ye shall **not surely die***" (*Gen.3:4; cf. 2:17*), rebutting God's primary statement.

The sequel to the conversation between Eve and the serpent is well known. She yielded to the temptation and fell from her own steadfastness. In the process, she brought her husband into the transgression as well. Adam was not deceived even though he too had listened to the serpent's presentation (*1 Tim.2:14*). But because Eve "*took of the fruit thereof and did eat and gave also **unto her husband with her**,*" he did eat (*Gen.3:6*).

Some of the effects of eating the "forbidden" fruit were immediate. Eve willingly moved to tempt her husband. She seemed to have had no misgivings about persuading him to sin. She turned to Adam and invited him to eat also. But when Adam ate of the fruit, everything changed. Both he and Eve now saw the world around them in a completely different light. Their life centers had shifted from the spiritual to the carnal. Their nakedness became a matter of shame. They took steps to conceal their bodies from one another.

Reviewing again the circumstances of the fall, there is no indication that Eve was attempting to "get even" with God. She had no knowledge of good and evil. The Bible simply says that she was deceived (*1 Tim.2:14*). She herself conceded as much later on. Eve openly admitted to God that, "*the serpent beguiled me*" (*Gen.3:13*). But, while she was taking a stand and owning up to her fault, her husband Adam was attempting to avoid blame. He explained that he had sinned because of "*the woman whom*" God had given him (*Gen.3:12*).

But, the fall could not be reversed. Its consequences could not be annulled. As a result of the fall of man, the foundations of authority established by God were turned upside down. The changed natures of Adam and Eve took them in directions contrary to God's will and purpose. Even the garden itself was no longer a place of harmony and fellowship with God. They were expelled. But, before they were evicted, God Himself moved to provide them with a reprieve. He made coats of skins to clothe them by covering their nakedness. God also provided a way of continued access to Himself though the shedding of blood.

Yet even, the fall could not hinder the plans and purposes of God for man. It simply opened the door to another way. The events leading up to it took place before Adam and Eve had any knowledge of good or evil. Their obedience was not meant to be dependent upon their personal judgment of what was either right or wrong. The idea was that God required them to obey Him because of faith in His Word.

Obedience to the Word of God continues to provide the moral and spiritual framework that is necessary for resisting the serpent (Roms.10:17). But their responses to the temptation revealed the unique characteristics of the man and the woman. There are elements within the woman that make her distinctly female same for maleness in the man. Apart from their physical differences, women and men continue to be different in a variety of ways. But, each is fitted to his/her natural role. Hidden traits in each of them drive their attitudes toward God's Word and each other.

Eve is often described as the "*weaker vessel*" (*1 Pet.3:7*). But she was the primary actor in taking the initiative and "breaking rank" with God. Also in their responses to God after the fall, she seemed more willing than the man to take responsibility for her behavior. Eve was not reluctant to give leadership to the man. But her responses were not congruent with her role. The Bible describes her behavior as usurpation of authority (*1 Tim.2:12*).

Once outside of Eden Adam and Eve were confronted with the task of providing for their own needs. They were assigned to God's "alternative-to-life" plan. The impulses of the flesh had become significantly aggravated. They were now under the influence of sin. It is not surprising to find that Cain their firstborn inherited a similar spirit of rebellion against God.

The ravages of "death" continued to have echoes in the lives of Adam and Eve in spite of their best efforts. Making a way for themselves in the world left much to be desired. The earth was cursed and resisted the efforts of man and the blessings of childbirth became a painful burden for Eve as she struggled under male rule. Even the privilege of sacrifice as a means of communicating with God could not replace the bliss of life in Eden.

It is certain that Adam and Eve communicated a knowledge of God to their children. Both Cain and Abel were involved in worship and made sacrifices to God. But the nature of sin in man is not easily reconciled. Cain their firstborn continued in a path of total rebellion.

Despite all of the burdensome initiatives necessary to sustain life, it seems that Eve continued to experience seasons of rejoicing with God. She had exercised disappointment and pain over the loss of her two sons. But now she rejoiced again at the birth of Seth. Like Abel, his name was associated with Divine worship. The Bible says that after the birth of the son of Seth, *"began men to call upon the name of the Lord"* (*Gen.4:25, 26*).

But the descendants of Adam were now divided into two groups, those who were righteous and those who were unrighteous. Before long, the effects of sin began to touch the lives of all men. The drift away from God intensified. Preachers of righteousness arose, even Enoch and Noah. But, the sons of God themselves even the righteous men of that day, were seduced by the sensuous appeal of the women around them. Sin was transforming the entire race of men.

The changed perceptions of Adam and Eve, an impact on all men. The presence of sin continued to redefine sexual distinctions and sexual roles also. Men and women no longer saw themselves as God saw them. The meaning of "maleness" and "femaleness" had become blurred. The process of disobedience continued to overturn the natural order that God had put in place at the beginning.

In the course of time, women began to find alternatives to male authority. As one retraces the history of women in the scriptures, that tendency seemed to predominate. Without directly challenging the authority of Jehovah, they kept on striving to change the hierarchy of authority, which God had established on earth (*1 Cor.11:3ff*). It is not surprising to find in the New Testament a warning to all with respect to the woman usurping the authority of the man (*1 Tim.2:12*).

Increasingly, women had begun to chafe under the dominance that was reducing them to a state of near servitude in many places. Rebellion against the authority of the man followed as naturally as night follows day. The tendency to resist authority which first manifested itself in Eve continued to find expression in many societies as the overriding influence of sin kept on turning the world upside down.

The struggle for women's "rights" had its beginning soon after the fall. As early as the days of Abram and Sarai the contest with Hagar put the spotlight on aspects of it. Secular history and Bible history are full of relevant instances. The daughters of Eve who have been considered in this study were no different from women everywhere. They too were driven by what seemed to be in their best interests. A classic case is that of Athaliah who even murdered her own grandchildren in order to pursue her selfish ambitions (*2 Ki.11:1-3*).

Significant changes came at Pentecost too with implications that were worldwide. God's relationship with man was dramatically altered. But these changes did not overturn the creation status of men and women. The Second Adam had come, had conquered sin and death, and had returned to heaven. But at His departure, He reminded His disciples that He would send the Comforter; that is the Holy Spirit (*Jn.16:7*). In addition, He had commanded them that, "*they should not depart from*

Jerusalem, but wait for the promise of the Father" (*Acts 1:4*). The Divine presence of Jehovah, even God's Holy Spirit had come to dwell among men according to the promise of the Father as articulated by the Son (*Acts 2:1*). This event marked a revolution in the affairs of all men and women everywhere.

Gentile believers brought new patterns of living to communities that were essentially Jewish. Conflicts were bound to arise. Within this new frame-of-reference, the changed roles of women became more evident. Their involvement in services of worship offered new challenges. In many respects, the door to the perceived liberation of women was now opened.

The Church and Pentecost brought much relief to many women who were formerly excluded from significant participation in worship. It also introduced distinct changes in the relationships between men and women who were believers. But in the process questions of God's authority vis-à-vis man's authority kept on creating obstacles. There began to arise a tendency to give way to the rule of men as a substitute for the rule of God.

Pentecost had given a new impetus to the rising revolution of women against the authority of the man. The Women's Liberation Movement, which took form in the twentieth century, came into its own. It defined the roles of women in terms of the roles of men. It assumed that equality between the sexes could only be adequately expressed in the sameness of duties and responsibilities. This position has brought about a significant misunderstanding of the rights of men and women as God defined them. In short order, the movement soon acquired political muscle. It began to exert pressure on governmental agencies to review the status of the woman in every area of life. As women moved in increasing numbers from the home to the workplace, family life itself was redefined and all of society was caught up in a revolution of roles.

History itself bears witness to the early legitimate struggles of women for identity. The Old Testament record examined the plight of the daughters of Zelophehad with respect to their rights of inheritance and the steps which had to be taken to change the law (*Num.27:1-11*). This situation became even more evident when matters arose concerning separation or divorce. But, in the meantime, there were other significant women who were "making waves," and breaking with tradition, creating new role models for the women who followed them.

As one reviews again the women of Noah's day, they had completely broken with tradition. It would seem that feminine modesty was cast aside. It is likely that Isaiah was referring to a comparable situation when he described the women of his day. He spoke of the rings and earrings and leg ornaments and nose jewelry that they wore. He also described their walk, "*with stretched out necks and wanton eyes, walking and mincing as they go*" (*Isa.3:16*). Could it be that these were the conditions, which swept the men of Noah's day away from their own steadfastness? The Bible reminds all men that "*as it was in the days Noe, so shall it be...*" (*Lk.17:26*). It is safe to say that the times of Noah are upon us.

Changing conditions in the larger society of men have strongly influenced the roles of women in the church too. The impact of social change has become more significant in the church than the authority of the Word of God. With consistency the scriptures themselves are being reinterpreted in ways that bring its teachings into conformity with the will of men.

One needs to be reminded, that there must be no yielding to the tendency to usurp the authority of God in the church (*1 Tim.2:12*). The Bible warns that "*in the last days perilous times shall come. For men shall be lovers of their ownselves...having a form of godliness but denying the power thereof*" (*2 Tim.3:1-5*). God's authority to rule in the church must remain unchanged. Church government is based on the model of a theocracy not a democracy. Jesus Christ is Lord (the Second Adam) and He is the Head of the church (*1 Cor.15:45, 47*).

The laws of God are not to be arbitrarily changed because of man's misuse or abuse of them. This principle applies to all of God's laws including God's natural laws. The laws of authority with respect to men and women are no exception. They are designed to facilitate the best interests of both not a distorted perception of those interests. God's principles continue to be man's only source of valid authority. To contradict them is to continue to create an environment that is alien to the will and purpose of God.

An overview of the *Legacy of Eve* brings into view a wide range of issues. But, all reflect a common theme, the striving for freedom from the authority of man. Like Eve today's women pursue what seems to be in their best interests without regard to outcomes. Quite often issues are cited which refer to the material progress of the modern woman, but overlook the negative impact on the morals and manners of the human society as a whole.

The simple homemaker whose ideas and aspirations often remained buried in the home now has a voice in the affairs of men. But all of society pays a price. Women now occupy many of the influential positions in world affairs, in business, in politics, in research, and in every walk of life. But society the world over will continue to be affected negatively until the home becomes significant again. Today both women and men seem to be turning away from their God-given mandate. The rise of self-interest above duty has been at the root of much child abuse and other social disorders.

There is no denying that men have played a dominant role in the struggle for survival on the planet. They have been inventors, explorers, rulers of nations, and in every aspect of living they have had primary responsibility for giving direction and exercising leadership. By comparison the roles that have been played by women have tended to be more supportive and behind the scenes, but equally significant. Even in times of war, women have often been in the background, maintaining life at home and providing support for the men in the frontline of the battle. But increasingly, women have become more aggressive in the pursuit of "Rights." For them equality is often measured only in terms of sameness of opportunity with the man.

There are two events described in the Book of Revelation, which summarize the full *Legacy of Eve*. In the first instance, it seems that the nation of Israel is portrayed in Heaven as a woman, wearing a crown of Twelve Stars (*Rev.12:1*). She conceived and brought forth a man-child *"who was to rule all nations with a rod of iron"* (*Rev.12:5*). Many scholars associate this woman with Mary Magdalene the mother of Jesus. Some religions even refer to her as the "Queen of Heaven." This trend is considered by some theologians to fit into the prophecy of Jeremiah. He identifies the nation of Israel as the Wife of God (*Jer.3:20*).

The Church also is often described in similar terms. The Bible speaks of it as the Bride of Christ and many are invited to the Marriage Supper of the Lamb (*Rev.19:7*). Such a picture portrays the Legacy of Eve as that which has become the symbol of salvation for all men.

In the second instance, there is a woman who is identified as *"The Great Whore that sitteth upon many waters"* (*Rev.17:1*). She was labeled *"The Mother of Harlots"* (*Rev.17:5*). She is described as the one who corrupted the earth with her fornication (*Rev.19:2*). She is presented as the highest manifestation of all that is morally evil in the world. The sexual revolution of Noah's day and the times in which we live present another face of Eve's Legacy.

But, as a general rule, Eve's legacy in its fullest manifestations emphasizes the characteristics of the fallen woman who establishes her own sense of what is appropriate for her. In this regard, the attitudes of women continue to shape and reshape the terms and conditions of living for all men. Particularly in recent times, women have been the primary movers in designing and redesigning the moral climate. The entertainment industry also and the range of public commercials all set a tone that highlight the woman as an object of sensuous delight.

All things considered, it seems that the daughters of Eve will continue to strive to remake and modify their environment to conform to their perception of equality and personal freedom. This drive to control her own destiny does not submit easily to the authority of God. It sets aside the principle of waiting on God to bring to pass what is in the best interests of men and takes control in its own hands. In the anxiety to "have it her way" the woman sets aside every "hindrance" and makes "her way" the frame-of-reference for living. This is the downside to the *Legacy of Eve*.

The current state of affairs in today's world makes it easier for women to gain public sympathy for any acceptable cause. But, there is reason to believe that the aggressive thrust of today's woman to compete with and gain dominance over the man is not within the best interests of any society. This tendency has always been active and alive, subversive at times, but never dead. This is the common bond that has united all women down through the ages. This is the foundation for the primary *Legacy of Eve*.

Unisex public facilities, interchange of male-female roles in marriage, feminizing of male attire (earrings, nose rings, necklaces, hairstyles), and a general neutralizing of distinctions in gender have significantly influenced how men are perceived by themselves and by others. To add to these concerns, changes in the role of motherhood have reduced the time allotted for the healthy maturation of the child. Childhood nurture has been redesigned. Children too have authority for making premature decisions and neutralizing the ability of parents to discipline them.

All such systems tend to undo the moral "glue" that is necessary for maintaining an intact social order. To make the difference the message of the church must be reaffirmed to reflect the completeness of God's

Divine revelation. Efforts must be made to amend the negative elements in Eve's Legacy.

The tendency of the woman to usurp has also introduced disorder in the church. It moves to disrupt God's hierarchy of authority. By way of example, the recommendation of a head covering for women spoken of in the scriptures is meant to be a signal of the willingness of the woman to continue to recognize God's order. The *Legacy of Eve* to all women in many respects poses a threat to the authority of God even in the church. All systems are indicating that the entire world has come under the influence of negative elements in the *Legacy of Eve*. It even drives men and women to set aside the authority of God and prioritize the authority of the woman.

The Bible says of these times, *"that in the last days perilous times shall come. For men shall be lovers of their own selves"* (2 Tim.3:1, 2). The Lord Jesus Himself observed that *"as it was in the days of Noe, so shall it be also in the days of the Son of man"* (Lk.17:26). But many apostasies tend to involve irregularities in the relationships between men and women that violate the bonds of one fleshing.

The question may be asked, "How did our world come to this place?" It is evident that the sustained Legacy of Eve has not been one of submission to, or acceptance of male headship. Her initiatives in the Garden were primarily disobedience to the authority of God. However, reference is made in the book of Proverbs to the sustained "strength" of the man, which may or may not be given to the woman. If the authority of the man has been compromised, then like Adam it is because he has conceded it.

As one reviews the history of man the Bible presents a fairly clear perspective on the living conditions along the way that contributed to the present state of affairs. As early as the days of Cain the impact of sin began to take its toll on the nature of man made in the image of God. The sin of Cain led the way but others soon began to follow. Lamech boasted of his sexual liberty living in a manner that was contrary to the Will of God (*Gen.4:19*). Before long, the whole world was in chaos as men and women reached out each to establish his/her own way.

In the course of time, women became more assertive and in many societies, men abdicated their role of leadership. The Book of Judges calls to mind the exploits of a woman named Deborah. She was a prophetess in Israel. She had commissioned Barak to gather an army to fight against the enemy. But he said "*if thou wilt go with me then I will go; but if thou wilt not go with me then I will not go*" (*Judg.4:8*). The Women's Movement born in our times is an outgrowth of the struggle against male dominance often combined with the irresponsibility of men. But, none of these conditions provide justification for any violations of the creation status of men and women.

There can be no doubt that the church will be the ultimate testing ground for questions around male authority. In an article in <u>Time</u> Magazine (November 23, 1992. p53), entitled, "The Second Reformation," the statement is made that "admission to the priesthood is just one issue as feminism rapidly emerges as the most vexing thorn for Christianity." But, the entire range of feminine issues in our day really revolves around the authority of God vis-à-vis the authority of man and the laws of an Unchanging God in an ever-changing world.

When God created man in His own image, He did not make mistakes. The true identities of the man and of the woman are properly determined by God alone. Every effort must be made to resist any Legacy that turns the world upside down and puts the rule of men in place of the Authority of God. There is a genuine fear that this warning has come too late for this present generation. All the evidence seems to indicate that iniquity will continue to abound and many believers will fall away from the faith. It is likely that Satan will eventually have his way with Eve completely after all. All things considered, the primary *Legacy of Eve* will eventually provide the gateway to rebellion against God, and the pathway to salvation through Jesus Christ.

Dr. Roderick Loney

ABOUT THE AUTHOR

Roderick Loney is the Pastor of Beth'aleel Fundamental Baptist Church in San Fernando, Trinidad and Tobago, where he maintains voluntary ministries to the larger community.

He is a graduate of Moody Bible Institute and earned a B.A. in Bible Archaeology and M.A. in Church History from Wheaton College. At Columbia University, he completed a Doctor of Education (Ed. D.) and a Ph.D. in Stress Management Psychology at Clayton University.

He is also the author of -

Bible Reflections: Journeys of the mind
The Sabbath as Salvation
The Inner Faces of Mercy

www.ingramcontent.com/pod-product-compliance
Lightning Source LLC
LaVergne TN
LVHW051830080426
835512LV00018B/2806